Your Towns and Cities in the

The
Isles of Scilly
in the Great War

To Jamie, Commodore
Royal Navy – who held
the service Nosetter for
over 40 years.
With deepest respect.

Richard Lawn. 20·11·2017

To Bridget,
my rock, thank you for your patience

*   *   *

Books concerning the Isles of Scilly by the author and co-authors

Sir Cloudisley Shovell's Disaster in the Isles of Scilly, October 1707, 1985
Admiral Shovell's Treasure and Shipwreck in the Isles of Scilly, 1999
Cornish Shipwrecks – the Isles of Scilly, 1971, 1975, 1979
Shipwrecks of the Isles of Scilly, 1993, 1995
The Cita – Scillies' Own Whisky Galore Shipwreck, 1997, 1998
Ships, Shipwrecks and Maritime Incidents Around the Isles of Scilly,
    (Museum Pub) 1999
A Diver Guide – Dive the Isles of Scilly and North Cornwall, 2003, 2006
Poor England has lost so many Men (Isles of Scilly Council Publication),
    2007
Augustus John Smith – Emperor and King of Scilly, 2013
*Built on Scilly – the history of shipbuilding on the islands between 1774-
    1891*, 2013
The Wrecks of Scilly, 2010, 2015

Your Towns and Cities in the Great War

The
Isles of Scilly
in the Great War

Richard Larn OBE

Pen & Sword
MILITARY

First published in Great Britain in 2017 by
PEN & SWORD MILITARY
an imprint of
Pen and Sword Books Ltd
47 Church Street
Barnsley
South Yorkshire S70 2AS

ISBN 978 1 47386 766 6

A CIP record for this book is available from the British Library

Printed and bound in England
by CPI Group (UK) Ltd, Croydon, CR0 4YY

Typeset in Times New Roman by Chic Graphics

Pen & Sword Books Ltd incorporates the imprints of
Pen & Sword Archaeology, Atlas, Aviation, Battleground, Discovery,
Family History, History, Maritime, Military, Naval, Politics, Railways,
Select, Social History, Transport, True Crime, Claymore Press,
Frontline Books, Leo Cooper, Praetorian Press, Remember When,
Seaforth Publishing and Wharncliffe.

For a complete list of Pen and Sword titles please contact
Pen and Sword Books Limited
47 Church Street, Barnsley, South Yorkshire, S70 2AS, England
E-mail: enquiries@pen-and-sword.co.uk
Website: www.pen-and-sword.co.uk

Contents

Acknowledgements

The author acknowledges with thanks and appreciation, the co-operation and support of the many individuals and organisations who have made material and photographs available and helped in the preparation of this book, including:

Amanda Martin, Chairman of the Council of the Isles of Scilly and Curator of the St Mary's Museum, for her introduction, proof reading and supply of photographs from the museum's collection; Judy Douglas, Assistant Curator; the late John Osborne, editor of a *Scillonian War Diary 1914-18*; Katie Herbert, Curator/Deputy Director, Penlee House Gallery and Museum, for photographs from the Percy Sharp Collection; Imperial War Museum; National Maritime Museum; Barbara Cuthbert, Curator, Fleet Air Arm Museum; Redruth Cornish Studies Library; John and Kate Banfield; Roger Banfield; David Duncan; Colin Mumford; Keith Low; John Dart; John and Jean Goodie; Mike Harcum; Richie Christopher; Chris Peat and David McBride for IT support; Sarah McBride; and my wife Bridget Larn for her research assistance and endless patience.

Foreword

DUCHY *of* CORNWALL

10 BUCKINGHAM GATE   LONDON SW1E 6LA
Telephone: 020-7834 7346   Facsimile: 020-7931 9541

Foreword from the Duchy of Cornwall

'The Isles of Scilly in the Great War'

This book has been very well researched on the important role fulfilled by the Isles of Scilly in the Great War of 1914 to 1918. Owned by the Duchy of Cornwall for almost 600 years at that time, it is gratifying to think that such good use was made of these strategically significant Islands. We must all thank the 500 Island men (from a total population of 2000) who served our country and mourn the 46 who were lost.

My congratulations to Richard Larn on a worthwhile and fascinating book.

Alastair Martin
Secretary and Keeper of the Records
Duchy of Cornwall

May 2017

Introduction

Twenty-eight miles south-west of Land's End, the Isles of Scilly stand guard like granite sentinels on the periphery of the Atlantic Ocean. These tiny islands have had an important role in the monitoring and defence of the Western Approaches since the sixteenth century.

The Great War (1914–1918) introduced many changes to Scilly. Hitherto, any form of national or international conflict had been fought on land or at sea. For the first time warfare became both submerged and airborne. The Royal Naval Air Service flying boats and seaplane base on Tresco served to complement the activities of the Royal Naval Auxiliary Patrol Service, its Admiralty tugs, armed trawlers and drifters in their struggle to rid the seas of enemy submarines. Despite their strategic and military significance the islands were not merely the temporary home of soldiers, sailors and airmen. Local families sent their sons and daughters to support the war effort. On the various memorial monuments around the islands the Rolls of Honour testify to the sacrifice made by Scillonians.

In this book, Richard Larn has shown the dual aspect of the First World War in Scilly. His extensive research has furthered our understanding of naval and military tactics, whereas his long acquaintance with islanders has enabled him to illustrate the personal and domestic facets of war.

Amanda Martin
Chairman of the Council of the Isles of Scilly
and Curator of the St Mary's Museum

Prologue

When Great Britain went to war with Germany in 1914, the government made two assumptions, one being that the war would be over in a matter of months, the other that we would win. No one could have envisaged that the war would last for more than four years, nor that so many lives would be lost; that the conflict would involve the entire world and that this country would come uncomfortably close to starvation. At the turn of the twentieth century, Great Britain had become complacent that its navy was invincible, sufficiently large to dominate the world if necessary, despite the fact a number of other countries aspired to emulate Britain and become colonial powers, including Germany, Japan, Russia, France, Italy, Austria and the USA. In order to achieve this Germany in particular required a navy the equal of ours, which by 1910 had twenty-two Dreadnought battleships, twenty-two pre-Dreadnought battleships, fourteen battle-cruisers, 160 cruisers and destroyers and eighty-six submarines.

Britain's military advisors were unfortunately at odds with each other to the detriment of both the Army and the Navy. Field Marshals were convinced there was still a place for cavalry in a modern army, oblivious of the havoc that could be wreaked by machine guns. They neglected to consider protective steel helmets for the army until 1916, sending troops into battle wearing soft uniform caps, despite Germany having had them from the outset and our Allies by 1915. The British Army was not alone in antiquated thinking, French troops fought the Germans in 1914 wearing bright red trousers, a blue tunic with a red-topped kepi cap, whilst the town of Verdun, France, thought impregnable with its twenty surrounding forts and forty redoubts, was in fact mostly armed with historic muzzle-loading cannon!

At home, many of our admirals had refused to accept that our fleet of battleships was already redundant, the submarine being the obvious capital ship of the future. Rear Admiral Wilson, the Third Sea Lord, in 1914 wrote: *'The submarine is an underhand form of warfare and a damned un-English weapon.'* Admiral Lord Beresford, aged 43, who led the Admiralty clique hostile to the 73-year old First Sea Lord 'Jackie' Fisher, due to a personal humiliating experience he had suffered at Fisher's hands twelve years earlier in Malta, supported Wilson, remarking: *'submarines were a waste of money and resources'*, whilst the Comptroller of the Admiralty confidently added: *'submarines would never be any use in war'*.

In opposition, Admiral John Fisher, a maverick who embraced innovation and technology, was adamant that the Royal Navy needed at least a hundred submarines as soon as practicable and was supported by the senior gunnery officer in the Royal Navy, Admiral Sir Percy Scott, who in 1914 expressed the view: *'The aircraft and the submarine have doomed that great floating gun-carriage, the battleship, to extinction.'*

Another example of blinkered attitudes to change was the Admiralty's initial dismissal of aircraft. In answer to the Wright brothers' offer of patents in 1907 for their aircraft inventions, they responded: *'Their Lordships are of the opinion that aeroplanes would not be of any practical use to the Naval Service'*, yet only two years later voted £35,000 to build a rigid airship, and by 1914 had a Royal Naval Air Service with its own aircraft, personnel and air stations.

Great Britain went to war with eighty-six boats (submarines are referred to as boats, not ships) whilst Germany initially had only twenty-nine and did not start its huge submarine building programme until 1916, convinced the war would be short lived. From the outset, the Admiralty assumed any naval involvement would be confined to surface fleets in the North Sea, so both countries laid vast mine-fields, one of which caused the first shipping casualty of the war the SS *Tysla*, a Norwegian ship of 4,676 tons, sunk off Flushing on 7 August 1914. By the end of the year German submarines and mines had sunk eighty-six ships in the North Sea, including the cruiser HMS *Pathfinder*, torpedoed by *U-21* on 5 September 1914, whilst *U-9* sank three armoured cruisers in one day, HMS *Aboukir, Hogue* and *Cressy*, on 22 September.

Naval policy was that the British Royal Navy's Grand Fleet would blockade the German coast, seal off the North Sea and take on the German *Hochseeflotte* based at Wilhelmshaven and ports in Heligoland, should they chose to venture out and fight. Meanwhile, Harwich was stuffed with destroyers, torpedo boats, light cruisers and submarines to escort the British Expeditionary Force (BEF) across the Channel in August and intercept any German units attempting to use the Dover Straits to reach the Channel. During the autumn of 1914 the Belgian ports of Ostend and Zeebrugge fell into German hands. By February 1915, evading extensive British minefields and nets in the Dover Straits by hugging the French coast, U-boats (a derivation of their German name *Unterseeboot* or submarine) entered the English Channel for the first time, sinking the SS *Oakby* off Folkstone on 23 February, then the SS *Branksome Chine* six miles off Beachy Head.

Fortunately, in anticipation of enemy submarines operating in the Channel and the Western Approaches, the Admiralty was able to augment a plan for the Royal Naval Auxiliary Patrol Service (RNAPS) to operate initially out of North Sea ports and later west country bases at Plymouth, Falmouth, the Isles of Scilly and Milford Haven. In 1907 Admiral Beresford first suggested that fishing trawlers and drifters could be utilized in time of war as minesweepers, armed patrol vessels, tenders and examination vessels. In 1909 the Admiralty opened discussions with trawler owners to charter eighty vessels in the event of war, later increasing that number to 150. To ensure trained crews were available if needed, a division of the Royal Navy Reserve (RNR) known as the Trawler Section was set up, and fishermen between the ages of 25 and 45 could sign up for periods between five and twenty years for which they received an annual retainer. They attended two weeks of Royal Navy training a year and were given equal status to Royal Navy ranks either as seamen on deck or engineers, trawler skippers/owners being made commissioned warrant officers. Hence a pool of professionally trained trawler crews and ships was ready and waiting for war. These fishing vessels were reliable sea boats designed to spend long periods at sea, were cheap to buy or hire and available in large numbers, ideally suited for this purpose.

On 4 August 1914 orders were immediately sent to 150 trawlers to cease fishing and proceed to designated dockyards for conversion. Many of them, trawlers in particular, were painted battleship grey, armed with small deck guns and fitted with wireless. Their huge coal bunkers were reduced in size to become mess decks, generating rooms or stores, after which they hoisted the white ensign and went to war. Trawlers over 100 tons were fitted with 12-pounder guns on the forecastle and often a smaller 3- or 6-pounder

A typical armed trawler of the Royal Naval Auxiliary Service. *(Richard Larn Collection)*

quick firing gun aft. Vessels under 100 tons, mostly drifters, were left painted black and initially unarmed or else given a small forecastle 3-pounder gun which was virtually useless due to its short firing range. Their roles were designated officially as patrol/mine sweepers, net drifters, boom defence, examination vessels or simply patrol boats. Lowestoft was the principal RNAPS base on the east coast, from whence trawlers patrolled the North Sea. Sixteen trawlers were lost by mines or wrecked in 1914, a total of sixty-six in UK waters alone in 1915.

On 3 August 1914, the day before Britain declared war, the army was ordered to mobilize. Six days later the Army Council ordered four divisions of British troops to France, resulting in 150,000 men of the British Expeditionary Force (BEF) being transported across the Channel on 17 August. Fortunately for Britain, Chief of the German General Staff Helmuth von Moltke rejected the proposal that the German High Seas Fleet should put to sea and attack them, saying: *'he would prefer to settle with them on land, the more English dead the better.'*

On 22 August the BEF and German cavalry clashed and actually fought each other with swords and lances at the Battle of the Marne, followed by the Race to the Sea and finally entrenchment.

This was the background to the Isles of Scilly's involvement in the First World War, which was minimal until 1915 when the islands came face to face with the reality of all-out war. There was no U-boat activity around the Scillies in 1914. In 1915 thirty ships were sunk off the islands, thirty-four in 1916 and forty-four in 1917, which brought about the need for a RNAPS base on St Mary's and later a Royal Naval Air Station on Tresco. Fifteen more ships were torpedoed in 1918, making a total of some 123, many of which received assistance from the Royal Navy based at St Mary's, who sent out armed escorts, rescue tugs or aircraft.

As to the number of volunteers from the Scillies who served in the armed forces, the total is an educated guess, since there is some uncertainty regarding how many Scillonian men lost their lives in the Great War. The council minutes for 6 February 1915 record that

A Royal Naval Air Service Lieutenant Observer in a SS.Z class airship stationed at RNAS Mullion, Cornwall, hand aiming and dropping a small bomb on a German U-Boat. *(Imperial War Museum)*

a *'Special Committee should make and maintain a list of the names of Scillonians taking part in the war against Germany and Austria since 1914.'*

The means of obtaining names and the definition of 'Scillonian' were freely discussed in council which resolved that the list might be divided into three parts: (1) Scillonians living in Scilly, called up or enlisted; (2) Scillonians living in other places, called up or enlisted who had parents residing on the islands; and (3) other men living on Scilly, called up or enlisted.

A list of Coastguards and Naval Reservists on active service was also requested. Dr Addison, the only general practitioner on the islands, was asked for the names of all volunteers who were medically examined by him prior to enlistment. There is no reason to believe that such a list was not maintained throughout the war, but what became of it is regrettably not known. Fortunately, the Chaplain of the Isles, the Rev. R. Bosanquet, assisted by the Rev.

C. Matthews of St Agnes, the Rev. J. Boyer of Tresco and Bryher and the Rev. W. Fookes of St Martin's, recorded in the Isles of Scilly Church Magazine a Roll of Honour, being the names of the men serving or killed in the Great War, which we have to accept as being accurate.

A poignant reference to the war appeared in the magazine in August 1914:

> *'There will no doubt be many sad occurrences during the war; we are likely to hear of some reverses and perhaps the loss of some of our ships; but we must not, therefore, get discouraged. In any war there are varying fortunes, and we must simply be resolutely determined to fight steadily onward. We have not sought this war, it has, it seems, been brought upon us by a gross violation of signed treaties, and to have stood on one side would have been cowardice; we must therefore trust the God who knows our earnest desire for peace will help us to bring everything to a satisfactory conclusion for us. Both Scillonians and Coastguards have been called up for Active Service; we can feel that we have a real interest in the movements of many ships. May God protect them and bring them safe home to us again.'*

In January 1917, the Reverend Bosanquet announced that for economic reasons and paper shortages the church magazine would cease to be published, copies having previously been delivered to every house on the islands. Fortunately, someone on St Agnes, possibly the Reverend Matthews, took up the challenge, managing to find some paper, and the magazine continued to be produced at least until the December 1918 issue, which included the Roll of Honour. Started around 1904, this magazine is the nearest the Isles of Scilly ever got to a 'newspaper', the islands relying on the telegraph, the mail, Cornish newspapers and word of mouth for news.

CHAPTER 1

1914
It will all be over by Christmas

'At first there will be increased slaughter on so terrible a scale as to render it impossible to get troops to push the battle to a decisive issue. Everybody will be entrenched in the next war; the spade will be as indispensable to the soldier as his rifle.'
Jan Bloch from *The War of the Future*, 1898

In 1914 no one could have foreseen the important and vital role that the Isles of Scilly would eventually play in the Great War. Owned by the Duchy of Cornwall and lying 29 miles out into the Atlantic west of Land's End, Cornwall, literally the most westerly part of England, the five inhabited islands of Scilly had little to offer other than flower farming. With no manufacturing capability, no industry, no minerals or coal, no mains electricity or water supply, no gas, no hospital, no wireless station (although there was a telegraphy cable linked to Land's End), no railway, no rivers, no canals, only nine miles of half-made road and a population of some 2,000 people – smaller than the average mainland village – the islands seemingly had little to offer the nation in time of war. However, the Isles of

Scilly had one important strategic advantage, which was their location.

This had been recognised and exploited by sailing ships from the 1300s, since the islands lay conveniently at the hub of six major shipping routes: transatlantic, the Bay of Biscay, the English and Bristol Channels, St George's Channel and the Irish Sea. Hence in the days of sail Scilly was literally a ship 'park', where vessels could generally lay safely at anchor awaiting a favourable wind, take on fresh water, re-victual or effect repairs. The Admiralty had long recognised this haven at the mouth of the English Channel and planned to exploit the Scillies' location in the mid-1800s by building a huge breakwater linking the islands of Samson and St Agnes. This would have created a protected anchorage not subject to the wind restrictions for leaving harbour experienced at Devonport and Plymouth and assisted men o'war employed in blockading French ports.

Some fifty men of the 105th Detachment Company, Royal Garrison Artillery, sent to Scilly in 1902-3 to install many new gun batteries on the Garrison. Here they are resting outside the Garrison Gate, having dragged a six-inch breech loading gun barrel from the Town Quay up the hill past Tregarthen's Hotel. *(Archaeological & Archival Mainmast)*

Temporary tented accommodation for soldiers of the 105th Detachment Co. Royal Garrison Artillery, erected on the Garrison field 1902-3, whilst more permanent accommodation blocks were being built. *(Mike Harcum Collection)*

Overlooked by Star Castle on St Mary's and its Garrison Wall with over 100 cannon, the anchorage would have been as secure as Plymouth Sound but in the end proved cost prohibitive and was never built. However, a different scheme proposed in 1898, at a time when Great Britain foresaw France as a future enemy, was completed at a cost of £250,000, only to be abandoned just seven years later.

This saw the construction of three huge naval batteries, each holding two 6-inch guns, along with two smaller quick-firing gun emplacements, protected range finding lookouts, searchlights and a full supporting complex of administration, engineering and accommodation buildings for a unit of the Royal Garrison Artillery (RGA). It even had its own underground electrical generating power station. Completed by the Redruth builder Arthur Carkeel in 1905, it was armed, commissioned and fully manned. Regular test firings at fixed targets on Samson and towed targets at sea then took place.

The Admiralty was informed that its Channel Fleet now had an alternative anchorage in the Western Approaches. Then Britain and France agreed that Germany was their future common enemy, an *entente cordiale* between them was signed, and at a stroke a Royal Navy anchorage at Scilly was no longer necessary. Hence the guns, shells, cordite charges, equipment and stores were all removed and the soldiers of the Garrison Artillery departed, leaving the islands with some 5,000 tons of redundant concrete structures and a derelict empty underground power station, now unfortunately without any generating capability.

It is quite remarkable, inexplicable even, that at the outbreak of the First World War those 6-inch guns and the overall complex were not reinstated to defend the islands. It was less than seven years since the guns had been taken away; even their mounting bolts wrapped in oiled cloth had not yet acquired a coating of rust, meaning that at minimal cost the islands would have protection from any German naval or military assault. Certainly, when in 1915 the Admiralty decided the Isles of Scilly should became a sub-base Royal Naval Auxiliary Patrol Station (RNAPS), reinstatement of the power station would have been most beneficial, since the islands were still totally reliant on oil, carbide/acetylene lamps or candles! Three diesel-driven generators and a new underground cable run

The Elizabethan Star Castle on the Garrison, St Mary's, built 1593. Used during WWI as a military headquarters. *(Richard Larn Collection)*

An impression of one of the four six inch breech loading guns mounted on the Garrison, in twin emplacements, showing the forged steel shield protecting the gun's crew. By 1912 these guns had been removed. *(Archaeological & Archival Mainmast)*

from Colonel Boscawen's battery on the Garrison to the quay on St Mary's would have made a huge difference to the supporting workshops and twenty armed trawlers and drifters which eventually comprised the RNAPS.

Whilst there may have been problems with the Duchy of Cornwall, who owned all the land and buildings on the islands, the Defence of the Realm Act, introduced by Parliament on 27 November 1914, virtually gave the Army and Navy absolute control over buildings and property considered necessary for war use. Perhaps the Duchy and the Council of the Isles of Scilly did discuss the possibility of the power station's reinstatement, but no evidence of this has been found in council minutes. It was 1931 before two Scillonians, Messrs. Nance and Sydney built a private Hugh Town generating station in the disused Worsall's quarry off Hoopers Hill, now Church Road, inviting the council and residents prepared to pay, to have their property connected.

On 23 June 1914, six weeks before war was declared, the islands had a foretaste of dealing with mass shipwreck survivors when the Belgian 7,660 ton liner SS *Gothland* ran ashore on the Crim Rocks at night, close to the Bishop lighthouse, whilst carrying Belgian undesirables deported from the United States. On passage from

Montreal to Rotterdam, she carried 131 crew, 86 passengers and a general cargo. Both lifeboats on Scilly and the packet vessel SS *Lyonesse* went to assist, survivors being taken off the ship and transferred to the larger vessels, St Mary's lifeboat saving eighty-one, the St Agnes boat seventy-one. All 217 survivors landed on St Mary's at midnight and were cared for by the Council of the Isles of Scilly in the Town Hall until taken to Penzance on the *Lyonesse*, the liner eventually being refloated and towed to Southampton where she was scrapped.

From August 1914 onward the Town Hall on St Mary's was deluged with government orders and instructions regarding war, aliens, Defence of the Realm Act, the possibility of air raids, travel restrictions, economy of food and coal and recruiting, yet these war

The historic gunpowder store on the Garrison built in the early 1600s for Star Castle, designated early in WWI as a public air raid shelter, and later used to store Royal Navy and Military explosives. *(Richard Larn Collection)*

topics are hardly mentioned in the council's minutes for the entire period 1914-18, despite what must have been a sizeable additional work load on council staff and cost.

An amusing anecdote published in the *Cornishman* newspaper on 14 August 1914, was the question Lord Kitchener asked of the porter as he entered the War Office to take up his new post as Chief of Staff for the first time. *'Is there a bed here?'* he asked. *'No, my Lord,'* the porter replied, *'we don't have beds in the War Office'. 'Then get one,'* said Kitchener, striding off to his office – a truly Churchillian touch!

A Government poster issued to all Councils to encourage the public not to waste food. *(Imperial War Museum)*

As in the rest of Great Britain there was a call for volunteers to join the armed forces. The new Minister of War, Field Marshal Lord Kitchener, convinced that the war would be a long one, wanted to recruit a 'new army' to supplement the professional soldiers of the British Expeditionary Force (BEF) and the part-time soldiers of the Territorial Force. However, with no recruiting office on Scilly, volunteers – and there were plenty of them – had to travel to Penzance to join up. All men on the islands between 18 and 45 were asked to attest if they would join up when wanted. To this end a national register of everyone between the ages of 15 and 65 was created, each issued with a registration or identity card. There was also a call for older men to volunteer as special constables, to relieve officers who had been on duty all day.

Scilly already had numerous sons and fathers in the armed forces and on the very day war was declared, when the light cruiser HMS *Doris* visited St Mary's and anchored in the Roads, 1st class Petty Officer William Phillips, who was on board, was allowed shore leave to visit his family. The next day, the cruisers HMS *Doris* and *Isis* captured the first two prizes of war, German three-masted schooners named *Bolivar* and *Roland*, carrying hides, tallow, coffee and tobacco leaf, whose crews were totally unaware that Germany and Great Britain were at war. Left anchored in St Mary's Roads, having had their sails confiscated, they retained their lifeboats, but three days later it was discovered that four of the *Bolivar*'s crew had made off through Broad Sound in one of them during the night. Whilst many locals predicted that the four German sailors would be drowned due to rough sea conditions, on 10 August, the *Western Evening Herald* printed the following news item.

GERMAN FUGITIVES PICKED UP AT SEA
'*A steamer of 700-tons, the New Pioneer, owned by the Co-op Wholesale Society, arrived in the Mersey having on board four German prisoners. The men were picked up in St George's Channel in an open boat in an exhausted condition through lack of food, and were brought ashore under armed guard.*'

On 11 August the two prize schooners were towed away by the cruiser HMS *Talbot*, bringing to an end the first incident of the First World War to affect the islands.

It is believed that Arnold Nance and his brother Arthur were the first two Scillonians to volunteer for Kitchener's Army. Other men known to be serving from Scilly included Sergeant William Cornish Phillips, who joined the Devon and Cornwall Light Infantry (DCLI) at the age of 16 in 1912 and fought with the BEF. By late 1918 he had been wounded five times, in France and in Mesopotamia. Sydney Elvin, another local boy who joined the Royal Marines in 1912, served nineteen years before discharge.

Others included Joseph Goddard who was in France for four years, whilst Samuel Somerford, George Green, Walter Ryan, James Jenkins, John Gambelli, Darius Hounsell, Thomas Summers, Albert Plummer, George White, Francis Darrington, William Phillips and William Woodcock had all joined the Royal Navy. Some of them, having been coastguards, were already warrant officers, chief or petty officers. Harry Webber had left the islands in 1914 to help build munition storage sheds at Woolwich Arsenal, then joined the Royal Navy and was on board the four-funnel cruiser HMS *Ariadne* when she was torpedoed off Beachy Head, fortunately saved along with Able Seaman William Phillips, another Scillonian, but some fifty men were unfortunately lost. Arthur Williams, of Telegraph, St Mary's, also joined the Royal Navy in 1911, serving for twenty-five years, to become a chief petty officer telegraphist.

Late in 1914 the Government declared a deserters' amnesty, which encouraged James Thomas Lethbridge of St Mary's to come forward and be pardoned. Born in 1862, his mother was a Woodcock, one of twins born on Samson Island. On leaving school he joined the Merchant Navy, and was bos'un of a four-masted Cape Horn barque by the time he was 19. He then found himself in the army after accepting the Queen's shilling following a serious drinking session. According to the date on his Egyptian campaign medal, he had fought in the Egyptian Campaign at Tel-el-Kebir early in 1914. Here he saw so much slaughter he deserted, walking 90 miles south to Port Tewfik, where the Suez Canal joins the Red Sea. From there he found a ship that took him to the Pacific and simply disappeared for two years. Confident his desertion had long been forgotten, he found his way back to Scilly, where his mother almost fainted when they came face to face, thinking she had seen a ghost. He simply kept quiet about what he had done, until he heard about the pardon scheme, receiving his at the Star Castle military HQ on St Mary's, when he was

Private Ralph Gluyas Banfield, of Holy Vale, St Mary's, who emigrated to Australia in 1913, joining the Anzac Army 1st Battalion Infantry, 4th Machine Gun Brigade in 1914. He fought in Gallipoli where he was shot in the head, then evacuated to England for treatment. (*John & Kay Banfield, Isles of Scilly*)

The Admiralty steam driven Trot Boat sent to St Mary's early in WWI to service the trawlers and drifters of the Royal Navy Auxiliary Patrol Service (RNAPS) stationed here 1915-18. *(St Mary's Museum, Isles of Scilly)*

ordered to join the crew of the Trot Boat, a twin-screw steam-driven naval harbour launch that ferried men and supplies out to vessels in St Mary's Roads which were moored to a string of 'trot' buoys off Newman House laid by the Royal Navy. James Lethbridge's family made a significant contribution to the war, since his six sons all joined up, five in the navy, the other living in Australia, joining the ANZAC army, all six surviving the war.

Full blackout regulations were introduced on the islands as a whole that October. There was great concern when a German Zeppelin airship, some 650ft long, capable of carrying 27 tons of bombs, flew overhead apparently taking photographs, since no bombs were dropped. At the same time the Government announced that in the event of air raids, church bells were to be rung to warn the public to take shelter.

An interesting entry in the diary of Annie Doris Banfield of Penzance in late 1914, whose father owned the West Cornwall Steamship Co Ltd, comments that 'everyone is knitting', which would have been the Scillonian ladies' contribution to 'comforts for the troops' – thick woollen socks, scarves and balaclava helmets to wear in the trenches during the forthcoming winter.

The most prominent family on Scilly in 1914 were the Dorrien-Smiths, who from 1834 held the lease of all the islands from the Duchy of Cornwall, but relinquished their responsibility in 1920 leaving them with just the lease of Tresco island. The family did not hear about the declaration of war on 4 August until 2 o'clock the following morning, and immediately arranged for a Trinity House vessel to call and take Arthur and Edward Dorrien-Smith to the mainland so they could join their Rifle Brigade and Shropshire Light Infantry units respectively. Lieutenant Thomas Algernon Dorrien-Smith, the lease holder of Tresco Estate, now having both sons in the army, said he was not willing to have four daughters idle at home, so whilst Innis, his 'right hand man', who helped run the estate remained on Tresco, Gwendoline was sent to Plymouth to train as a probationary nurse, whilst sisters Cicely and Charlotte went to Ashridge hospital, initially as cooks. All three sisters were advised by the War Office in reply to their letter *that ladies are not allowed to take their maids with them!'*

A prominent member of the family was General Sir Horace Dorrien-Smith, who was in command of the BEF's II Corps. He became something of a hero having saved the day for the British after the Battle of Mons by digging in at Le Cateau, but he was not to everyone's taste it seems. The *Cornishman* newspaper, quoting an unabashed subaltern, recorded:

> *'Everyone is utterly sick of Smith-Dorrien's name. His virtues nauseated us.*
> *At the club after a particularly heavy bombardment of Smith-Dorrien's excellences, a rather testy old gentleman said, to hear him talk one would think that Smith-Dorrien was God Almighty!'*

The eldest brother of six, Algernon, who had been a lieutenant in the 10th Hussars until he inherited the lease of the Isles of Scilly from his uncle, Augustus John Smith in 1873, sacrificed his military career in order to run his late uncle's estate. He was expected to add

'Smith' to his surname Dorrien, becoming Smith-Dorrien but eventually Dorrien-Smith. His brother General Sir Horace survived the Great War and in 1918 was made Governor of Gibraltar.

An act of generosity on the part of the Dorrien-Smith family concerned the Dorrien-Smith steamship *Lyonesse* which was the islands' supply line with the mainland. It operated out of Penzance carrying passengers and freight daily, especially boxes of flowers in season, the islands' only export apart from potatoes. Shortly after war was declared, the managing owner of the West Cornwall SS Co Ltd, told the council he would be obliged to stop running the ship since the underwriters carrying the insurance had said they were no longer prepared to insure the vessel due to the risk of its being torpedoed. For several months the chairman of the council had done his best to induce the Admiralty to run the *Lyonesse*, as it was impossible for him as owner to run the vessel at a loss. The owner of the vessel then offered a subsidy of £500 per annum towards the insurance premium, which in addition to the Post Office subsidy, the government's offer of £200, the Duchy of Cornwall's £100 and the council's £100 still left them £300 short of the Admiralty's terms. Eventually, the Dorrien-Smith family paid the additional sum themselves, which caused the council to record its thanks to them for securing continuance of the ferry service and for their assistance in providing such a large proportion of the money required.

Late in 1914, in addition to Lord Kitchener's appeal for 100,000 volunteers to join the army, a target exceeded by the end of September, the Government introduced a scheme to raise Defence Volunteer Units to defend the coast against possible German invasion, an organisation similar to the Defence Volunteers or Home Guard organisation of the Second World War. Whilst in many mainland areas there were problems in getting these men uniforms and weapons, somehow Thomas Dorrien-Smith used his influence to get his Scillonian volunteers everything they needed at an early stage, including Lee Enfield .303 rifles and bayonets. By December 1914 under his watchful eye and that of Major C.B. Maggs, Church Lads' Brigade (CLB), who was the Duchy of Cornwall's land

Twenty-nine Officers and other ranks of the Isles of Scilly Defence volunteers, similar to the Local Defence Volunteers (LDV) which changed its identity to the Home Guard in WW2. *(St Mary's Museum, Isles of Scilly)*

steward, they paraded and drilled outside Star Castle on a regular basis. They were even able to obtain a supply of Morris Tubes, small calibre 'liners' for the .303 inch rifles, enabling them to use smaller and much cheaper .230 inch bullets for target practice. When it was rumoured that a German U-boat was waiting close inshore to sink the *Lyonesse* ferry, a coastguard armed with a Lee Enfield rifle was put ashore on Great Arthur Island to keep watch for it by day. How he was to communicate with St Mary's if he saw anything, and what use a rifle would be against a submarine was not explained.

By late October some fifty soldiers were drafted to St Mary's, mostly men from the 3rd (Special Reserve) Battalion of the Devonshire Regiment who, backed up by local Defence Volunteers guarded what were considered important military installations, i.e. Star Castle, the quay and, by the end of 1914, the newly established

Royal Navy wireless station on Telegraph Hill close to the Coastguard Tower. Most of these were regular soldiers either convalescing from wounds incurred with the BEF or else were close to retirement age. Some lived on the Garrison in barrack blocks, others were billeted with local families, who received a welcome additional allowance of 9d a night per soldier, with an extra 7½d if breakfast was provided. A similar amount was offered for lunch and 4½d for supper, making a total of 2s 4½d per day for full board. It is perhaps worth noting that on 19 November, Mr Asquith, the Prime Minister, advised Parliament that the war was already costing between £900,000 and £1 million a day. At the Isles of Scilly Council meeting on 19 December, a rare reference to the war

Lloyd's Signal Station situated on the Garrison. Built as a windmill, then converted to a gun tower in Napoleonic times, playing a vital role in WWI passing shipping information to Lloyd's of London. *(St Mary's Museum, Isles of Scilly)*

appeared in the minutes, *'that a Committee had been appointed to keep a register of all Scillonians serving in HM Forces, and that framed copies were to be hung in the Town Hall and Council Chamber for the public to read.'* Unfortunately, no trace of that record has been found to date, or any of the posters, so that as mentioned earlier, Scilly has no official record of local men who served in the forces.

One of the early local casualties of the war was Eldred Cole Banfield of Holy Vale. He enlisted with the 1st/14th (County of London) Battalion of the London Scottish Regiment, as a private, and was killed in action 1 November 1914, aged 19. Having no known grave, he is commemorated on the Ypres Menin Gate Memorial, panel 54. Also of Holy Vale and part of the Banfield family was Ralph Gluyas Banfield, who had emigrated to Australia in 1913. In November 1914 he joined the Australian army as a private with the 11th Infantry, 4th Machine Gun Brigade, was sent to Cairo for training and then on to Gallipoli. Two years later he was shot in the head and sent back to England to hospital where he had a steel plate inserted. He made a full recovery, fought in France, went back to Australia where

Private Eldred Cole Banfield of Holy Vale, St Mary's. London Scottish Regiment, 14th Battalion, killed in action 1 November 1914, aged 19. *(Kay & John Banfield)*

he married a local girl and in 1924 returned to Scilly at his father's request to run the family farm which he did until he died, aged 44, in 1937.

Two weeks before Christmas 1914, over 10–12 December, heavy cruisers of the German High Seas Fleet closed on the east coast of Great Britain and commenced a bombardment of the towns of Scarborough and Whitby, firing some 1,500 shells into the towns, killing 127 civilians. Later, shelling of Shanklin and Sandown on the Isle of Wight debunked Admiral Earl Jellicoe's earlier public statement that *'the Isle of Wight was the safest place in the world!'*

A story emerged at some time during the war that the reason for the Isles of Scilly being neither bombed nor shelled was due to the Kaiser's appreciation of what the islands had done to assist German passengers and crew when the liner SS *Schiller* was wrecked close to the Bishop Rock in May 1875. Whether this is true or not remains uncertain and there appears to be no proof either way. Zeppelin airships later bombed Lowestoft and Great Yarmouth, a prelude to six German airships dropping 50lb bombs on Bury St Edmonds in May 1915. This was something of a wake-up call for the country as a whole, especially Scilly, which had no hospital and only the one medical practitioner, Dr William Addison. He ran both a medical and dental practice and acted as the local Lifeboat Secretary from the basement of his home 'Fernleigh', today the Bell Rock Hotel. The local Red Cross Society was already preparing for emergencies. A large empty private house, Lemon Hall, named after the senior

Lemon Hall, Church Street, St Mary's, a private residence requisitioned as a naval hospital in WWI. *(Richard Larn Collection)*

ENG.LIEUT.COM SPENCE   D⁺ JOY   ENG.COM. WILLIAMSON

LIEUT.HINMAN   LIEUT.COM.LIVINGSTON

Royal Navy officers in Jack's Bar, Holgates Hotel, St Mary's. *(St Mary's Museum, Isles of Scilly)*

customs officer who had it built, which was located opposite the doctor's practice in Church Road, was requisitioned as a naval hospital, Dorothy Lovell and Dorothy McFarland being amongst the first recruited nurses.

Later, Holgate's Hotel on the Strand was requisitioned as both a hospital and service accommodation for the navy. The islands' council must have been acutely aware that German warships could lie off Porthcressa and Old Town Bay and bombard Hugh Town and Old Town, as well as Star Castle and the main harbour, which could have made St Mary's untenable. Instructions were therefore given that in the event of a Zeppelin raid or enemy surface bombardment, residents living in the west of Hugh Town should take shelter in the old Garrison Powder Magazine, whilst those living in the east should use the open fields off Moorwell Lane.

In addition to the Defence Volunteers, the government called for a Coast Watch organisation and by December twelve men had been recruited on St Mary's. Regular night patrols commenced in February 1915, working in three shifts of four men at a time, six hours on followed by twelve hours off. Two huts offering some shelter were erected, one at Tolls Hill, the other at Giant's Castle, the men being required to walk the coastal path between Toll's Island and Giant's Castle from dusk to dawn looking for signs of any unusual boat activity, such as lights at sea or anyone attempting to land on the beaches. St Agnes and Bryher had a similar organisation with a Royal Navy petty officer appointed to supervise. Apparently, the St Mary's watchers were ordered to pay particular attention to Deep Point, where a telegraph cable

Nurse Major of St Mary's, who worked in the hospitals throughout WWI. *(St Mary's Museum, Isles of Scilly)*

connected to the wireless station came ashore from Land's End, in addition to the nineteenth-century cable that came ashore at Porthcressa. Unlike many areas of the mainland, none of the Scillies' beaches were mined, cordoned off with barbed wire or had restricted public access imposed, hence they were safe to patrol.

Since most of the coast watchers were past their prime, each patrol was allocated a boy as a runner, capable of getting urgent messages initially to Star Castle, but later after the RNAPS base was established in 1915, to the Royal Naval Headquarters at the White House on the Garrison. The boys did this for seven days and then had a week off serving as signal station runners for the Marconi Wireless Station at Telegraph Hill. The boys chosen were in their last six months of school, considered sufficiently educated to justify leaving at 13^1/$_2$ instead of 14. The men were paid 24s a week, the

Non-commissioned chief and petty officers of the RNAPS Staff, based at the White House. *(Penlee House Gallery & Museum, Percy Sharp Collection)*

boys 6s, which was good money compared to the 1s 1d per day a private soldier was paid fighting in France or Belgium.

An important feature of social life for boys on the Isles of Scilly at the time was the Church Lads' Brigade (CLB), part of a national male youth organisation that was a mix of religion, discipline and the military rolled into one, a branch of which had been started on St Mary's in 1905. The CLB promoted the habits of obedience, reverence, discipline, self-respect and all things considered necessary towards true Christian manliness. When on parade they wore a black suit, white shirt, black tie and a military style pill-box cap with chin strap, or else a dark school blazer, shirt and long trousers. Run on strict military lines, the CLB accepted recruits from as young as 5 years of age up to 18, who were taught carbine drill using dummy wooden rifles, physical exercise, mounting and relieving guards, signals and semaphore, in short preparing them for a career in the services should they so choose. Today its equivalent would be the Army Cadet Corps, and a national CLB organisation still exists today, now open to both sexes. The unit on

St Mary's even had its own fife, drum and bugle band, which led their parades and frequently performed in public. The local branch on the islands has long since closed.

Lord Kitchener launched an appeal on 7 August 1914 for 100,000 volunteers to join the armed forces, a target well exceeded by the end of September. Such was the enthusiasm and patriotism to join up and fight that over half a million young men came forward. By the end of

Private Alexander Farquharson Banfield, of Holy Vale, St Mary's Royal Horse Artillery, wounded and invalided out of the army. *(John & Kay Banfield)*

Group of the RNAPS Royal Navy officers, non-commissioned chief and petty officers, two Royal Marines and one Able Seaman who who worked at the White House Headquarters. *(St Mary's Museum, Isles of Scilly)*

December 1914, eighty-four men had left the islands to serve, nine of whom had already been killed in action. Five Scillonians – Michael O'Leary, Thomas Stevens, Hamley, Brewer and Dungay – lost their lives when HMS *Monmouth*, an armoured cruiser, was sunk along with HMS *Good Hope* on 1 November by the German battleship *Gneisenau* along with two other cruisers in the Battle of Coronel, off Chile in the Pacific. This was Britain's first major naval defeat for over 100 years and had a profound effect on the Admiralty.

Those five men, along with the previously mentioned Private Eldred Cole Banfield, in the 1st/14th London Scottish Regiment, were the first Scillonian casualties of the Great War, all having died on active service on the same day, all having no known grave. Those in the Royal Navy went down with their ship, whilst Private Banfield is not only commemorated on the Menin Gate Memorial, but also on a memorial window in Hugh Town's parish church. Their death on active service brought the government's feared telegram, following by a standard letter from the War Office or Admiralty, sent to every family who lost a relative.

Telegram: War Office, London.
'Deeply regret to inform you that (name of deceased, service unit or ship), was killed in action on (date). Lord Kitchener expresses his sympathy.'
Letter: Army Form B: 104-82
'Sir/Madam, It is my painful duty to inform you that a report has this day been received from the War Office notifying the death of: name; rank; regiment; location of casualty; date, and I am to express to you the sympathy and regret of the Army Council at your loss.

[NB: The cause of death was usually recorded as 'Killed in Action'.] *If any articles of private property left by the deceased are found, they will be forwarded to you but some time will probably elapse before their receipt and when received they cannot be disposed of until authority is received from the War Office. Applications regarding the disposal of any such personal effects, or of any amount that may eventually be found to be due to the late soldier's estate, should be addressed to: The Secretary, War Office, London, SW, and marked outside, "Effects".'*

A total of eighteen of the eighty-four Scillonians now in service had previously been members of the CLB and, with the Devon and Cornwall Light Infantry the county regiment, it is not surprising that twenty-three men from the islands had volunteered to serve with them, with many more to follow when conscription was introduced. Meanwhile, five local men who were with the BEF had been wounded.

Uniform cap badge of the Devon & Cornwall Light Infantry, the county Regiment many local men joined. *(Richard Larn Collection)*

The nearest recruiting office to the Isles of Scilly was on the mainland at Penzance, but according to the Islands' Council Minute Book No.3, 1911–1923, those men wishing to join up first undertook a medical examination in the Town Hall, the Army Medical Board having been given free use of the premises for the inspection of men of military age in the islands. They then made the frequently rough 39-mile sea crossing to Penzance before signing on. Along with many others, this was where Alfred George Phillips presented himself in September 1914, where the Recruiting Officer was paid 2s 6d per man enlisted (by today's values, some £6 per recruit). They were supposed to insist on a minimum height of 5ft 3ins, chest 34ins, and candidates to be at least 18 years of age to sign on, or 19 years of age if they wanted to fight overseas immediately after training. Generally recruiting offices turned a blind eye to age since very few of the applicants had birth certificates. There was also a degree of collusion throughout the recruiting process anyway, so as to get as many men and boys into uniform as soon as possible.

A quite remarkable story of a Scillonian soldier in the First World War concerned William Cornish Phillips, who left the family home

at Anglesea House, the Strand, to join the DCLI in 1912. Lance
Corporal Phillips was sent to France in August 1914, with what the
German Kaiser called the 'contemptible little army', along with
other Scillonians, Jack Ancock and Claude Phillips. During the
fighting, as a sniper, William was up a tree when a shell burst close
at hand and ruptured both of his eardrums. Promoted to sergeant,
he was at the Battle of Mons on 23 August when he was shot, the
bullet stopping just below his heart. He was shipped back to The
Mote Hospital in Maidstone, Kent, which was owned by Sir Marcus
Samuel Bt and his wife Dorothea who later became Viscountess
Bearstead. An operation to remove the bullet was considered so
dangerous that only the king's surgeon was capable of performing
it. Lady Bearstead offered to pay the surgeon and his expenses if he
would come down to Maidstone that day. The operation took place
at midnight and next day a photograph was taken of the soldier in
bed surrounded by the surgical team.

Lance Corporal William Phillips in a hospital bed with the medical team that
saved his life, after removing a bullet from close to his heart. *(John & Kay
Banfield)*

Three British 0.303inch bullets, part of another showing cordite sticks, and the actual German bullet head removed from William Phillips chest. These live rounds were found on the Somme battlefield by the author. *(Richard Larn Collection)*

WWI relics from the Somme. A German fused shell nose-cone, and a large piece of shrapnel. *(Richard Larn Collection)*

Private Claude Phillips, a former Church Lads' Brigade (CLB) member, was shot in the face, had a silver jawbone fitted and was sent back home to recuperate. Whilst transport was laid on for him on his return to Scilly on convalescent leave in the form of a gig and horse, to get him from the quay to his parent's home, a contingent of the CLB insisted on taking the place of the horse and pulled him from the quay to the Town Hall, where he received an official welcome home.

William Phillips, who arrived home on Scilly on medical leave a week later, had no such hero's welcome, but had to shoulder his military pack and walk! On recovery William was sent to Salonica as part of a scouting team going behind the Bulgarian lines to capture enemy officers for interrogation. During one of these patrols they came across a village where almost every inhabitant had had their throat cut or else been bayoneted. The sole survivor was an uninjured eight-year-old extremely traumatized little girl. William took her under his wing, getting his companions to cut off the tails of their shirts in order that one of them, a tailor by trade, could make her a dress. The little girl stayed with the soldiers for months, sharing their corned beef and biscuit rations, until eventually they found a convent which took her into their care. William was later bayoneted through the neck in a hand-to-hand skirmish and was sent to a hospital in Cyprus to recover.

When pronounced fit for service again he was shipped to Mesopotamia to fight the Turks, and was behind their lines blowing up railway tracks, stores and depots, when he was shot in the neck. He was in Bighi Hospital, Malta,

Sergeant William Cornish Phillips, of St Mary's, Isles of Scilly, with the little Serbian girl he saved and befriended until a nunnery took her in. *(John & Kay Banfield)*

receiving treatment when the war ended. At last he was sent home after five years of horrific fighting and injuries, receiving his discharge from the army on the Isle of Wight in 1919. William was mentioned in despatches, and his letter of commendation and service medals are now in the St Mary's Museum on the Isles of Scilly.

Concern by Councillor Ward regarding future island finances was expressed at a council meeting held only two days after war was declared: *'due to possible scarcity of money, all departments of the Council's work should be restricted as far as possible.'* In December a circular from the Home Office was distributed regarding the early closure of all shops in the Christmas week, whilst Councillor MacFarland again proposed the council keep a register of all Scillonians serving in the armed forces, a subject raised yet again in February 1915.

In the Magistrates Court on 17 October the clerk was directed to ascertain if the Isles of Scilly was a Prohibited Area under the Aliens Restricted Act 1914, as they were not included in the 2nd Schedule of place names in the Order made in Council, leaving members unclear as to what action the council should take. And so 1914 came to a close for Scilly, with no immediate threats to the population but no sign that hostilities would cease in the near future, Lord Kitchener having announced that in his opinion the war would last for at least three years while the Kaiser predicted that

TO DRESS EXTRAVAGANTLY IN WAR TIME IS WORSE THAN BAD FORM IT IS UNPATRIOTIC

Government poster issued in 1914 encouraging the public to be thrifty and modest in their dress. *(Imperial War Museum)*

'fighting would stop before the leaves have fallen off the trees.' It is worth noting that Kaiser Wilhelm was a grandson of Queen Victoria and was in fact an honorary Admiral of the Royal Navy!

In November decisions were made which was were to bring the Isles of Scilly into the forefront of the war at sea when Great Britain declared the whole of the North Sea a war zone. Any ships bringing contraband of war to German ports, including food, were liable to be taken as prize of war or sunk. In retaliation, Germany declared all the waters round the British Isles a war zone, in which all shipping, including neutral vessels, were liable to attack without warning. The plan was to blockade these islands and starve the population out, bringing the country and hence the British Empire to its knees, without having to prove superiority in a grand sea battle. This was a new and frightening development, literally a moment of history in naval warfare.

CHAPTER 2

1915
The war at sea comes to Scilly

It's not invasion we have to fear if our navy's beaten, it's starvation.

Rear Admiral 'Jackie' Fisher, 1890

The war of course did not end at Christmas and Lord Kitchener's prediction of at least three years of conflict was now beginning to seem a reality, but still Scilly was virtually unaffected. The Town Hall had been busy in the last quarter of 1914 issuing identity cards, creating hospitals, worrying about aliens and making war preparations as recommended by the Government.

U-boats were now beginning to operate further afield and for the first time, in January 1915, a German submarine, *U-21*, made its way down the English Channel and up the Irish Sea, sinking the SS *Ben Cruachan* and the barque *Linda Blanche* on 30 January off Liverpool. The following day two Royal Navy colliers, the SS *Turquoise* and *Nugget*, bound for the Dardanelles, were sunk close to Scilly by submarine gunfire. Their crew was fired on as they scrambled into the lifeboats, causing one man to be killed and eight wounded whilst the captain of the *Nugget*, who had remained

Armed trawler of the RNAPS, painted grey, with a 12pdr. 12cwt. gun mounted behind the funnel. *(Richard Larn Collection)*

aboard, attempted to ram the U-boat single handed. HM Trawler *Anthony Hope* raced to their rescue and picked up all the survivors.

It was March 1915 before the true reality of war struck home on Scilly. For four months the previous year German U-boats had observed the International Cruiser Rules, which allowed the crews of merchant ships to take to their boats before their ship was sunk, and for submarines to tow boats carrying survivors close to a friendly shore. Challenged ships were not allowed to fly false colours or that of a neutral country, nor aim a gun at a submarine or attempt to sink the enemy. This all came to an end when the SS *Phrygia* rammed and sank a U-boat, the Germans retaliating by *U-24* torpedoing the SS *Glitra* without warning off Norway, killing forty of her French crew. Now the gloves were off, international rules and agreements went out of the window and from 18 February

The SS *Headlands* sinking off the Bishop Rock, after she had been torpedoed. An unarmed drifter of RNAPS St Mary's is ready to take off the crew. *(Painting by the late Clive Carter)*

1915, Germany embarked on a submarine blockade of Great Britain, meaning any ship in British waters was liable to be sunk, regardless of flag.

On 12 March, *U-29* on patrol off Scilly torpedoed and sank three merchant ships in one day, the SS *Headlands, Indian City* and *Andalusian*. The former was challenged and forced to stop, then torpedoed once the crew had escaped. Hearsay has it that parents and school children gathered on Peninnis Head, St Mary's and clapped and cheered at the explosions and smoke, but since this happened 10 miles south of the Bishop Rock, it is unlikely they saw very much. The ship stayed afloat until the following day, drifting to within a mile of the Bishop lighthouse before foundering.

The *Indian City* was less than two months old when she fell victim to *U-29*. Carrying cotton and zinc, she had an all Chinese crew who severely tried the patience of Lieutenant Commander Otto von Weddigen, the submarine's commander, by making him wait whilst they all put on their best clothes and packed their bags before taking to the lifeboats. The crew of *U-29* never knew how close they came to annihilation that day. Having forced the Ellerman Line 2,349 ton British *Andalusian* to stop before setting their explosive scuttling charges, the Germans stripped the ship of cutlery, navigational instruments and charts. The British crew, having abandoned ship, were then ordered out of their boats and told to board the submarine and stand on her foredeck from where they witnessed their ship go down. It was not much consolation, but Captain Weddigen then handed out cigars to the survivors before they returned to their boats! Once the submarine had submerged, the crew of the *Andalusian* made for a nearby sailing ship which took them on board, the SS *Lyonesse* later taking the *Andalusian* in tow only for it to sink before she reached the islands.

The German submarine *U-29* coming up astern of the SS *Headlands* on 12 March 1915, after which the ship was torpedoed. (*St Mary's Museum*)

Unbeknown to *U-29*, she was within only a few miles of HMS *Antwerp* (ex *Vienna*), the second secret Q-ship, a small heavily armed merchant ship manned by the Royal Navy deliberately acting as a decoy vessel. On her first war patrol out of Falmouth, *Q-2* headed west towards Scilly looking for submarines. Originally a Great Eastern Railway steamer working the Harwich to the Hook of Holland route, she was now armed with two 12-pounder guns hidden from sight. At 3pm that day 12 miles north of the Bishop Rock lighthouse, Lieutenant Commander Herbert RN, spotted *U-29* on the surface some distance off, so deliberately went alongside the sailing ship carrying Captain Malley and his crew from the *Andalusian*, hoping to lure the enemy back to attack two vessels for the price of one. *Q-2* then broke away and went after the submarine getting to within four miles, but *U-29* was not to be drawn and submerged. She later met her end on 18 March in the North Sea, when she was rammed and sunk with all hands by the battleship HMS *Dreadnought*.

The surrendered German *UB-101* photographed on the surface in Mount's Bay, off St Michael's Mount in 1918. *(Penlee House Gallery & Museum, Percy Sharp Collection)*

On 13 March the *Lyonesse* docked in Penzance from Scilly with ninety-four survivors from the three torpedoed ships. Many of them were very drunk and two succeeded in falling into the harbour between the ferry and the quay. The next day a three-masted schooner, the *Louis Joseph* was brought into Penzance from Scilly by the coastguard vessel HMS *Squirrel*, suspected of supplying petrol to German submarines. She was supposed to be carrying canary seed, but her draught was too deep for such a light cargo and she was arrested and left with a dozen soldiers on deck with rifles and fixed bayonets to guard her crew. The *Squirrel* then brought in a second schooner, the *Biernais* of Bordeaux on 15 March. A telegram received on the mainland said that a submarine had landed the crew of a ship on Menawethan, one of the Scillies' Eastern Islands.

A remarkable 'mini-battle' between *U-28* (Captain Georg-Günther von Forstner) and the British SS *Vosges* made history on 27 March. Instead of obeying the submarine's signal to heave to and abandon ship off Land's End, Captain John Green, whose ship was bound for Cardiff, increased speed and commenced to fire rockets for assistance. The U-boat opened fire and one of the shells struck her bridge wounding several officers and killing one sailor. Captain Green then swung his ship from side to side, hoisted the red ensign as a sign he was prepared for battle and attempted to outrun the enemy, causing the U-boat to zig-zag whilst continuing to fire her 22-pounder deck gun. Heavy seas swept the submarine's casing causing more than one of her gunners to be washed overboard, life-lines allowing them to be recovered. For four hours the *Vosges* led the submarine in a deadly chase towards Scilly, whilst shell after shell hit the ship riddling her hull, starting several fires, the sea pouring in through numerous holes. Royal Navy destroyers then appeared and the U-boat broke off the engagement, submerged and made off, leaving the merchant ship to slowly sink and her crew to escape.

By mid-March the Coast Watchers on Scilly were well established, carrying out their nightly patrols on all the islands except Samson and Tresco. On St Mary's the head watchers were H. Ashford and D. Toomey, assisted by J. Phillips, W. Phillips, M. Nicholas, G. Phillips, W. Nance, J. Laffin, J. Jenkins, J. Pearce and

J. Bickford. The boys of the CLB who acted as runners were: J. Edwards, C. Guy, W. Perring, R. Bodilly, V. Trenwith, R. Thompson, with O. Pinsent in reserve.

On Bryher: Head Watcher R. Jenkins was in charge, his team being C. Jenkins, E. Jenkins and J. Pender. On St Agnes, Head Watcher F. Hicks was assisted by S. Hicks, R. Legg and W. Treneary, whilst on St Martin's the Head Watcher D. Skinner, was assisted by W. Ashford, E. Ashford and W. Osborne. There were now two telephones on Bryher which enabled the Coast Watchers there to report direct to Lloyd's Signal Tower on the Garrison (previously known as Bailey's Tower), who relayed any messages direct to the Admiralty via the telegraph cable, as well as to the White House on the Garrison.

The Defence Volunteers formed at the end of 1914 now numbered forty-five by 1 April 1915, their honorary commander being T.A. Dorrien-Smith, assisted by Captain Huxham, Lieutenant Maggs, Sergeant Major Watson and Sergeant Armourers E. Moyle and W. Hill, with Corporals S. Deason, J. Moyle and Lance Corporal J. Laffin. The privates were: H. Sanoney, E. McDonald, B. Banfield, C. Stideford, C. Jenkins, H. Trenwith, A. Guy, A.Thompson, R. Thomas, G. Thompson, A. Poynter, W. Webb, R. Thompson, A. Trenear, H. Mitchell, J. Ellis, W. Pender, A. Lethbridge, C. Morris, S. Watts, W. Guy, F. Pender, H. Bickford jnr, R. Stevenson, R. Penrose, W. Nance, M. Nicholas, H. Jenkins, H. Bickford, J. Phillips, W. Phillips, S. Phillips, D. Toomey, J. Pearce, J. Jenkins, H. Ashford and Medical Officer Dr W.B. Addison.

The Dorrien-Smith sisters who had gone to Ashbridge hospital in 1914 moved on to France, where they worked in the Rouen Station Coffee Shop, a canteen for British, French and Indian troops who were moving up the line from Le Havre, run by Lady Mabelle Egerton. The sisters then moved to No.10 Military Hospital, where Cicely caught measles which developed into bronchitis and then pneumonia, from which she died, aged 33. Charlotte, who also developed measles but recovered, accompanied her sister's body back to Scilly from Penzance on board the SS *Lyonesse* on 14 April, the coffin covered by a Union Jack sent over specially by her father. She was laid to rest in Tresco's churchyard, the flag left in place at her father's request. The inscription on the family gravestone reads *'Cicely Francis Dorrien-Smith, born 4 November 1882, gave her life in the service of her country at Rouen 18 April 1915'*.

Her three sisters, Edith, Gwendolen and Charlotte were, in the fullness of time, all buried in the same plot. Following Cicely's

The headstone of Cicely Dorrien-Smith and other members of her family in Tresco churchyard. *(Richard Larn Collection)*

funeral Charlotte and Gwendolen went on to Le Tréport, to the Lady Murray's Hospital which was attached to the Tenth French Army. This was turned over to the British later in 1916, the two girls going to a Belgian hospital at La Parma which had over 1,000 beds.

From 26 April an armed sentry was posted to guard the Garrison magazine building, which suggests it was now serving its original purpose, the storage of explosives, in which case it presumably was no longer a civilian air-raid shelter. No civilians on the islands were allowed to talk to shipwrecked sailors landed on Scilly in case they asked the name of their ship or where they were attacked. A Scillonian pilot was overheard to ask an officer from one of the crews landed on the quay something to do with his ship. He was immediately ordered by a sentry to report to the White House on the Garrison, the naval headquarters, where he was severely reprimanded. Armed soldiers on the quay who met every shipwrecked crew as they landed, escorted them to the Town Hall where they were questioned, registered, fed and accommodated until they could be shipped to Penzance on the *Lyonesse*, preventing any contact with the locals for security reasons. Naturally there were gossip and rumours and the locals were probably better informed than the authorities anyway!

The large RNAPS base at Falmouth, named HMS *Forte*, had to be established before Scilly could be set up. The exact date when either came into being is uncertain, the first reference to the Naval Base, Falmouth, in the Harbour Commissioners' Letter Books for example, being a communication to Captain Valentine Phillimore DSO RN, dated 15 March 1916, but HMS *Forte* is thought to have been established long before, possibly late 1914. Falmouth was the principal west-country Naval Patrol Base, which later had a vice admiral in charge, a large fleet of patrol vessels and control of Holman's Dry Dock in Penzance, used for repair work to trawlers and drifters based at St Mary's, Newlyn and Penzance.

Annie Banfield, who came from Penzance, but whose father was a Scillonian, kept a diary which mentions a Peterhead trawler on patrol duties entering Penzance harbour for orders on 11 February

The Headquarters Staff of RNAPS St Mary's, grouped outside the Garrison Gate. Included are seven Royal Navy Officers; three WRNS, two Royal Marines, two Petty Officers, one naval Rating and one soldier. (*St Mary's Museum*)

Top Row: L.Corpl. Hale, RM Not known, Sgt. Holmes, RM HQ. Orderly Naval Police
2nd row: WRNS. Ruby Stevenson, PO. John Geale, WRNS. PO. Noble, PO. Jim Landsbury, Pte. Vic Trenwith WRNS. ? Victualling Office Writer Messenger
3rd row: Sub. Lt. Bellier, Lieut. Slater, Lieut. Thompson, Captain Randall, Lieut. Bedell ? Warrant Officer Mr. P. ? Paymaster E.W.S. Officer 2nd i/c RNAPS Commanding Officer Paymaster

NB: The two WRNS ratings, were the daughters of the Isles of Scilly Customs Officer

1915, presumably based at Falmouth, and she mentions the Scillies' ferry having an encounter with another patrol vessel five days later. The *Lyonesse* was making regular daily crossings between the islands and Penzance, carrying military personnel, stores, civilians, food supplies, oil and ammunition, but was seemingly not recognised by HMS *Vienna*. The warship was a merchantman which had been converted into an armed boarding ship, decoy *Q-2*, mentioned earlier. On 16 February she stopped the ferry off Land's End and armed sailors actually boarded the *Lyonesse* making threatening gestures before they realised their mistake and withdrew.

It is reasonably certain that an embryonic St Mary's naval base was established late in 1914 since in a letter from T. Dorrien-Smith to the Duchy of Cornwall in December he wrote, *'in the interests of the Naval Base, passengers, mails and goods, the daily* Lyonesse *service should be maintained*,' whilst the islands' church magazine of December refers to *'patrol boats that can be called upon to go into immediate action'*. This brought a reprimand from the War Office reminding the editor of the need for national security, since it was known that the German government was reading British journals, magazines and newspapers.

From April 1915 onward there is a wealth of information concerning the war at sea around the islands and the RNAPS base on St Mary's which, interposed with extracts from Miss Banfield's diary and newspapers, gives a wider picture. On 1 April after gunfire was heard near the Bishop, Commander Oliver RN, senior commanding officer at St Mary's, sent the trawler *Fezenda* to investigate. That evening the *Carbineer* came in with Captain Venning and his twenty-four crew from the SS *Edale*, torpedoed nine miles north-west of the Bishop, which sank after nine shells from the submarine's 14-pounder gun were fired into her. Visiting St Mary's that week, Miss Banfield recorded that from Telegraph Hill on 2 April she could clearly see ten patrol vessels surrounding the American tanker SS *Gulflight* which had been torpedoed west of the Bishop whilst carrying a volatile cargo of naphtha, causing her crew to jump overboard.

Her captain, named Gunther, suffered a heart attack on the bridge and died, leaving the drifters *Lowestoft, Premier, Diadem, Primrose, Dusty Miller* and *All's Well* to tow her eight miles to the safety of St Mary's Roads. The patrol drifter *Iago* returned to Scilly with all thirty-five crew and the body of her captain, as well as two others who had drowned. The deceased were put into the mortuary

The United States tanker, SS *Gulflight,* torpedoed off Scilly but saved by armed trawlers and anchored off the Garrison. *(St Mary's Museum)*

building at the back of the quay. Three days later, Miss Banfield tells us she went out in a boat to look at the *Gulflight* and watch divers inspect her hull, and that a British destroyer arrived that day with Lieutenant Towers and Naval Constructor McBride, as well as US Navy and US Embassy staff to examine the vessel.

On 4 April HMS *Rovenska*, an armed patrol yacht, reported to the commander-in-chief (C-in-C) Falmouth by wireless telegraphy (W/T) that he had the crews of two steamships on board that had been torpedoed off Scilly, and was taking them direct to Penzance. W/T signals the same day at 10am from the SS *Anglo Californian* stated that she was under attack from a U-boat and that several crew members had been wounded by shell fire.

Establishing a naval base on St Mary's was no simple matter, which presented the Admiralty and the community with huge problems. The patrol trawlers and drifters, which grew in number to over twenty, with crews numbering some 300, required huge amounts of fresh water and coal for the ships' boilers, commodities that were in short supply on Scilly at the best of times. Accommodation had to be found for shore-based naval personnel as well as medical facilities and of course they had to be fed. The patrol boats were now landing survivors, many of them injured, from torpedoed ships almost on a daily basis. The White House on the Garrison, which had been requisitioned as the Naval Headquarters, accommodated the commanding officer, his WRNS secretariat, pay and administrative staff. Tregarthen's Hotel became the RN officers' wardroom where meals were taken and officers had bedrooms. It was also an emergency hospital. Bank House was the WRNS quarters, the two-storied building just inside the Garrison Gate becoming the victualling store and office. The present

The 'White House' on the Garrison, used as the headquarters of the RNAPS St Mary's, throughout WWI. The house was built for Master Gunner Abraham Tovey in the 1700s. *(Richard Larn Collection)*

Mermaid Inn, then a three-storied cargo warehouse built during the Scillies' shipbuilding era, was requisitioned by the Admiralty to store dry goods from ships undergoing repair, whilst Holgates Hotel accommodated and fed other naval personnel.

St Mary's quay underwent a transformation, with existing and new buildings used as stores, artificers' machine shops, blacksmith's shop, boiler-makers' shop, explosives stores for mines and ammunition as well as administrative offices and a mortuary. Naval colliers brought coal from south Wales in prodigious quantities, such as the SS *Prince Charles*, which arrived on 30 April with 300 tons, its cargo landed on the quay and stacked in huge piles. The armed trawlers, which remained at sea for four or five days at a time, constantly on the move, were expected to 'coal-ship' on return using their own crew, which was a filthy, back-breaking task. After days of severe gales at sea, heavy weather, escorting merchant ships and attacking U-boats, the men eventually revolted and refused this task, causing the Admiralty to recruit fifteen Welsh miners from Cardiff, who carried out the job until the end of hostilities. The futility of handling the coal twice, once onto the quay and then into the trawlers' bunkers was eventually alleviated by keeping the colliers at Scilly until empty, letting them go alongside any patrol vessel on the quay that required fuel, the miners shovelling it straight into their bunkers.

Solving the fresh water supply was not so easy, a problem that became a priority for both the Admiralty and the Island's Council, which had been debating the subject of drinking water since August 1897. Six councillors had visited the twelve main wells on St Mary's and sent samples away to the London Clinical Association for analysis, the results of which were neither encouraging nor acceptable:

'Not fit for drinking purposes; water of doubtful purity; not a good water and should be avoided if possible; too impure to be safe; could not be held desirable for use as drinking water etc.'

The wells in question all had names: Lenterverne well, Maypole, Carn Friars, both Old Town's new and old wells, Gemmy's, Sammy's, Ram's Valley, Well Cross, Aunt Joaney's, Moor well and Mr Watt's well. The council officer whose brief it was to keep an eye on sewage, water and general cleanliness had the rather strange title of 'Inspector of Nuisances'. He had an additional long-standing problem with the residents of Buzza Street, St Mary's, who habitually disposed of all their rubbish and dirty water onto the road, whilst others used Carn Thomas beach to get rid of their fire ash, rubbish and even human waste.

Years earlier in October 1897, the council had had a plan for improving the water supply on St Mary's, offering two schemes. Scheme One, involved the cleaning and deepening of existing wells and providing new wells with pumps and pipes laid into the town from Ram's Valley at an estimated cost of £265. Scheme Two, estimated at £790, would see a reservoir built on Buzza Hill, supplied from a Ram's Valley windmill pump, with pipes into the town and part way up Garrison Hill. This also offered drinking water

The present-day water reservoir situated on Buzza Hill, dating back to 1924, which replaced the original tanks erected by the Admiralty in 1915 to supply the fleet of RNAPS vessels. *(Richard Larn Collection)*

piped into private homes whose tenants were prepared to pay the connection charge and annual water rate. However, nothing was done until 1901 when Old Town received a storage cistern on Castle Rocks and pipework to supply the community.

The Royal Navy Base CO's weekly report to Falmouth on 29 April stated, *'during this week the water windmill has been completed and one or two trawlers have been watered; hoses have been demanded as those in use on the trawlers are very leaky and much water was wasted.'* As the war progressed, the water problem was eventually solved with the building of storage tanks and pipes laid to the quay, which necessitated a visit in May by Captain Phillimore DSO RN and Engineer Captain Perkins RN from Devonport, who looked into the whole question of the water supply.

On 7 May the Cunard liner SS *Lusitania* was sunk by *U-20* some 80 miles north of Scilly, causing the death of 1,198, of which 291 were women, 94 children and 124 American citizens. It was the largest loss of life from one ship in the war to date. Whilst the event did not affect Scilly, it later inspired the author Michael Morpurgo in 2015 to write *Listen to the Moon*, a novel in which a young girl on board the liner is picked up by *U-20* and dropped off on the Eastern Isles of Scilly.

That same day trawler No.1191 *Whitefriars* arrived at St Mary's from Portsmouth, boosting the number of patrol boats stationed at St Mary's to fifteen. The impact of an additional 250 navy patrol boatmen on such a small island was bringing behavioural problems. The Record Book of the Scillies' Court House 1835–1917 shows that at the Magistrates Court on 6 May, the proprietor of the Atlantic Hotel, Albert Poynter, complained that there was too much drunkenness amongst the crews of patrol vessels now stationed at the islands and considerable noise in the streets late in the evenings. The magistrates, T.A. Dorrien-Smith and William Gluyas, ordered that a notice be given that all five licensed premises which sold intoxicating liquors should in future close at 9 o'clock in the evening.

The trawlers *Diamond* and *Anthony Hope* joined Scilly from Devonport the same day; the *Cambria* was sent out to join Patrol

The entire fleet of some twenty armed trawlers and drifters which made up the RNAPS Base on St Mary's from early 1915. The larger vessels are colliers, which brought in coal for the fleet. *(St Mary's Museum)*

Unit 85, and that evening the two trawlers making up Unit 86 returned from sea, the men paid and two Royal Navy Engine Room Artificers joined the base to boost the shore-based workshop staff. The *Anthony Hope*'s skipper, new to Scilly, grounded her on Bacon Ledge whilst approaching the quay, remaining there for five hours and losing a blade from her propeller.

The shortage of fresh water continued, sometimes requiring patrol boats to go to Penzance, an 80-mile round trip just to fill up, which is what the *St Ives* was ordered to do on 18 May. That was the day the crew of HM Trawler *Iago* gave trouble whilst in Newlyn, although the weekly report to Falmouth on her return does not elaborate, simply saying:

> '*Sent the Carbineer to Penzance with prisoner J. Chearman from the trawler Iago for Bodmin Naval prison. Number of trawlers at St Mary's now sixteen. Patrols are now arranged so that vessels are at sea 4 to 5 days and in harbour 36 hours a week. Fusilier came in to land a signal boy who had hurt himself.*'

In response to an urgent plea from the British Army Medical Council for steel helmets, the army was finally issued with the Mk.1 Brodie steel helmet in 1915, patented by an Englishman, John Leopold Brodie, modelled on the original Cornish tin miner's helmet. It was immediately called the Tommy or shrapnel helmet, or simply the Tin Hat. Countless soldiers in the trenches had suffered head wounds as anti-personnel shells fired by the Germans exploded low overhead, scattering small lead balls downward like giant shot guns, the British regulation soft uniform peaked cap offering no protection at all.

A Cornish tin-miner wearing the mining helmet which served as a model for the first British Army tin-hat. The lump of clay holds a candle, each miner carrying his own illumination. *(Redruth Institute of Cornish Studies)*

By mid-summer 1915 the still embryonic Royal Naval Air Service (RNAS), which had been formed by the Admiralty in late 1914, arrived on St Mary's with one of its Kite Balloon Service observation craft. Observation balloons were nothing new, having been used by various armies for centuries, observers inside baskets slung below balloons having the advantage of height for spotting what the enemy were doing and later, following the invention of the telephone and radio, were able to direct gunfire. The balloon that arrived on St Mary's was initially stationed on the Garrison playing field, where it was tethered to huge concrete mooring blocks whilst it floated up to 300-400ft above the ground. However, as everyone living on St Mary's knows, the Garrison playing field is extremely exposed to the prevailing south-west wind, so the balloon was moved first to the Garrison tennis court then after a few months to a more sheltered field at Holy Vale, where concrete mooring blocks have since been found.

It was in 1911 that the British Balloon Detachment became the Air Balloon Battalion of the Royal Engineers, which was then handed over to the RNAS, since the government saw more use for

The Mk.1 Brodie steel helmet issued to all British and Commonwealth troops in 1915. Prior to their issue, troops fought in soft uniform peaked caps. *(Imperial War Museum)*

them floating high above battleships at sea where they could increase their horizon tenfold. The BEF had just one battalion of them when they landed in France in August 1914. Hydrogen filled, each balloon needed some forty-eight men trained as a team to handle them from their overnight moorings into the air, several hours aloft and then back down to earth, these naval personnel being accommodated at Ennor House and Holgates Hotel. Each balloon carried a wicker basket slung beneath it measuring 3ft x 5ft, which held two naval officer observers who went up equipped with thick woollens, two pairs of long range binoculars, two telephone handsets with cables clipped to the tethering wire, two special cameras with zoom lenses, four filled sandbags and two parachutes.

They often carried two special gas bags holding reserve hydrogen, which connected to the refill valves above the basket which, in conjunction with the sandbags, could maintain the balloon's buoyancy. No explanation has been found as to why the station was abandoned after just one summer in California Field on St Mary's. Perhaps the open sea some 10 miles to the west outside of the Bishop light where U-boats and steamships were to be found, was too far away for the balloonists to be of any real use. Holy Vale was also visited by a RNAS airship in 1915 and Lewis Hicks, a schoolboy living at Porthcressa, was an eye witness. As the airship descended its mooring lines were held by dozens of men, enabling the crew to climb down a short

A kite-balloon of the Royal Naval Air service, deployed for a short period at Holy Vale, St Mary's. *(Fleet Air Arm Museum)*

The basket slung beneath a kite-balloon that held two observers. *(Fleet Air Arm Museum)*

RNAS airship No.SS.Z.49, based at RNAS *Mullion*, on the Lizard peninsula, which frequently flew over the Isles of Scilly in WWI whilst on anti-submarine patrols. *(Penlee House Gallery & Museum, Percy Sharp Collection)*

rope ladder to reach the ground. This is the only known instance of an airship landing on St Mary's, although several others did so on Tresco whilst the air station was being established.

Surprisingly, since the ferry *Lyonesse* was such a small innocuous vessel, she was in fact armed, but the only mention is in Annie Banfield's diary. On 25 May she recorded:

> *'The steamer had been measured for a gun, and by 9 June the Lyonesse left Penzance with the 6-pounder gun more or less fixed up, and when she got back from Scilly a large platform was being built around the gun base.'*

On 11 June she left Penzance for firing trials and it is surprising they allowed civilian passengers to be present, even if Miss Banfield was the owner's daughter. The *Lyonesse* went out into Mount's Bay with Lieutenant McBrian RN and a gun-fitter from Falmouth on board, where her gun crew fired three rounds to port, then three to starboard at different ranges, first at three miles, then 800 yards, Miss Banfield commenting: *'the shot fell smoking, making a lovely splash. The report was very loud, but not sufficient to use cotton wool in one's ears. Mr Blair (the gun fitter), gave me a brass cartridge case, very heavy, some nine inches tall.'*

On the Home Front, the First Lord of the Admiralty, Sir Winston Churchill, was dismissed from his post by Prime Minister Asquith following the failure of the naval attack on the Dardanelles. During the forthcoming November he was dropped from the government altogether for the failure of the Gallipoli campaign.

On 3 June, three days before German Zeppelins carried out a devastating bombing attack on London and east coast ports in which airship *L-6* killed sixty-four civilians in a 20 minute attack, on St Mary's a radio SOS message was received from HMS *Demerara*, saying she was fighting off a U-boat by gunfire in Lat.50° 30′N, Long.07° 30′W. The patrol vessels *Fusilier, Carbineer, Marne* and *Iago* were sent to assist. At 10.30am coast watchers on Bryher reported that a large submarine showing a sail attached to her periscope to give her the appearance of a sailing vessel was 10 miles offshore. The coastguards in Telegraph Tower then reported that a U-boat which proved to be the *U-3* was circling the Belgian trawler *Delta* and firing shells into her. Fortunately, HM trawler *Dewsland* went out and rescued her eleven crew members after she was sunk.

The council received a letter from the commanding officer of the 3rd Devon Regiment troops on Scilly on 11 June, saying: *'I wish to heartily thank the good people of the Isles who so readily gave mattresses to our soldiers at Telegraph, and to Holgates Hotel for conveying them to Telegraph. Signed: 2nd Lieut A. Noon, 3rd Devons Detachment.'*

The weekly report made to C-in-C Falmouth commented, *'During the week the water tanks have progressed satisfactorily, and the engine pumps at Moorwell are in place. The engine workshop is progressing well and will be ready when the lathes arrive. Trawlers at St Mary's now eighteen.'*

For the week commencing 10 June, Falmouth was told that:

'The watering plant has progressed slowly and by next week I hope to supply all the trawlers with water. The process of filling the tanks is rather slow since on top of the hill (Buzza) it takes only half an hour to fill but two and a half hours to empty. Mr Thompson suggests a branch with a one and a half inch pipe from the church. Coaling is now satisfactory but necessary to keep up the supply of colliers; the eighteen trawlers are now using 400 tons a week. The watering is satisfactory, and five tons an hour has been put on board; the covering of the tanks has commenced which when full hold fifty four tons, and it will be some time before all four are covered but impossible to fill them until then. Sent an armed guard aboard Hercules IV to fetch a man named Anderson to be locked up for creating a disturbance on board. Trawlers here now twenty, and there are now four trawlers and a yacht fitted with Wireless Telegraphy.'

Meanwhile recruiting continued. The *Cornishman* newspaper commenting on the St Ives district, which included the Isles of Scilly, reported the islands' population as 7,984, and that 150 of its men were now serving (7.37 per cent of the population), with 60 more men eligible. That population figure was totally incorrect, a true figure being nearer 2,000.

The weekly report from the naval base to Falmouth on 30 June recorded:

'List of all twenty naval vessels stationed at St Mary's; No 1192 – St Ives; No 2659 – Kong Frederick; No 1361 – Hercules VI: No 1358 – Cambria; No 1359 - City of Edinburgh; No 1191 – Whitefriars; No 1376 – Diamond II; No 1579 – Emerald; No 1757 – Ottilie; No 2664 – Dewaland;

No 2662 – Hattano; No 1380 – Newbridge; No 1759 – Merrydale; No 1180 – Andrew Marvel; 1182 – Strathelliot; No 1360 – Nancy Hague.'

When it was announced that the police force were to receive a war bonus, there was much discontent, not only on Scilly but across the country as a whole. Individual finance committees granted a bonus to inspectors and all below that rank of 2s a week for married men and 1s 6d for single men, effective as of 1 May.

The trawlers at Scilly, which were much larger than the drifters, were not all equipped to the same standard, some being fitted with mine-sweeping gear, a few with W/T radio, some with only a 3-pounder forecastle gun, others with a more powerful 12-pounder. On 8 July HMT *St Ives* and *Hercules VI* were ordered to sea to sweep for German-moored contact mines reported off the Wolf Rock. Then at 1505 Commodore, Falmouth, reported mines laid in Lat 50° 19′N, Long 05° 52′W, and HMT *Whitefriars* and *Nancy*

The gun crew on an armed trawler at action stations. The weapon is a 6pdr.
(Imperial War Museum)

A WWI 12pdr. quick-firing deck gun, similar to the larger weapons fitted to armed trawlers of the RNAPS St Mary's, on display outside the Charlestown Shipwreck Centre, Cornwall. *(Richard Larn Collection)*

Hague were tasked with sweeping for them, with *Andrew Marvel* and *Merrydale* ordered to sweep square 80-QUC and report. That same day Commander Towers RN arrived on the *Lyonesse* to take charge of the St Mary's base in Commander Oliver's absence. On his return both men and Chief Petty Officer Carpenter Bennett inspected repairs to the steam launch *Endeavour*, along with Mr John Banfield of the West Cornwall Steamship Co Ltd. This launch, along with others, formed or constituted the Trot Boats, supplied by the Admiralty as general work boats, landing stores and men, taking crews out to the line of trot moorings specially laid in St Mary's Roads for the patrol trawlers and drifters, where they moored at night with their crews on board. There was a routine for the patrol vessels, depending on circumstances, which generally saw them at sea laying anti-submarine nets or escorting merchant ships for four or five days, then back in port for thirty-six hours, during which they had to coal and water ship, get paid, and effect any necessary repairs. Visits to the Falmouth Base were frequent, such as that made by Commander Oliver, Lieutenants Thomson and Millichap, and Engineman Rokhar on 11 July in drifter No.1869 *Girl Gracie*, to attend a disciplinary court hearing on skipper Peter Cormack.

Every ship sunk off Scilly had a story to tell and two incidents in particular are worth recording in some detail. The first was the sinking of the British SS *Caucasian* south-west of Scilly on 1 July. Outward bound for New Orleans with creosote, Captain Robinson averred it was *U-39* that fired seventeen shells into his ship, destroying the wheelhouse and steering gear before they hove-to. Whilst abandoning ship, the captain's dog, a Pomeranian named Betty, accidentally fell into the sea and started to swim towards the submarine. Its owner swam after it, put it on his back and was about to turn round when he realised *U-39* was close alongside. Her captain shouted at him that he had intended to machine-gun the boats for not stopping when ordered, but after watching the rescue of the dog had changed his mind.

Of all the incidents of ships stopped and sunk by U-boats around Scilly, the Norwegian barque *Fiery Cross* on 3 July 1915 was unusual to say the least, her captain having the temerity to demand a receipt from the U-boat for the loss of his ship! Stopped at sea and her crew ordered to abandon ship which was carrying oil from the United States, her captain told his crew to remain aboard whilst he rowed a dinghy across to the submarine, delaying the sinking of his ship by gun-fire for thirty minutes, whilst he asked for – and received – a receipt which read: *'I hereby certify that I have sunk the Fiery Cross, Captain John Geddie, on 3rd July 1915, at 3pm, as she had contraband on board, ie. lubricating oil for France. Signed: Forstman, Lieut Cdr'*, which was over stamped *'Imperial Marine, His Majesty's submarine U-'*, the actual number being erased.

On 15 July twelve Royal Navy drifters under Lieutenant Alix RNR, arrived at St Mary's on passage to Milford Haven. *Hercules IV*, based at St Mary's, had caught enough fish whilst on patrol for the entire Scillies fleet! That same day nine drifters went out to set

British 'horned' contact mine and sinker, which were laid in extensive 'fields' to protect harbour entrances and seal off channels used by U- boats. German mines similar to these were laid by surface ships or UB-Class submarines. *(Richard Larn Collection)*

up floating anti-submarine nets, testing an 84ft deep net for buoyancy.

The Scilly naval base was responsible for Patrol Area XIV, which also entailed Falmouth and Penzance vessels, the local vessels divided into Units 85, 87 and 92 consisting of three vessels each which patrolled together but had different armament. Twelve of them had the almost useless 3-pounder guns, two had 6-pounders, with only three the favoured long range 12-pounder guns.

Continuous demands were being made for better weapons to attack U-boats at greater range, but the armament factories had other priorities and it was much later before they were all suitably equipped.

On 28 July a new weapon was made available to the patrol boats at Scilly, depth charges, No.1361 *Hercules IV* being the first brought to the quay to have racks fitted. They had proved their worth earlier on 22 March, when *U-68* became the first submarine to be sunk by this new weapon. SS *Farnborough (Q-5)*, met up with her off Ireland, went through the charade of 'abandoning ship', then when the enemy drew closer the Royal Navy gunners used her three 12-pounder guns to shell the submarine hitting it several times. *Farnborough* then dropped a depth charge over the spot she had submerged, causing *U-68* to surface almost perpendicular. Two more charges finished her off and she went down with all thirty-eight crew. Lieutenant Commander Campbell, her CO, received a DSO, the crew £1,000 from the Admiralty to be shared between them. Later in the war patrol trawlers were fitted with 'bomb-throwers', anti-submarine mortar guns larger versions of the Stokes mortars issued to the army mid-1915. The naval mortar could throw a pressure sensitive 'bomb' some 500 yards, greatly increasing a trawler's firepower.

Meanwhile the problem of drunkenness on St Mary's continued to occupy St Mary's magistrates, who now sat almost every week. On 29 July, Joseph Jenkins, a local labourer, was charged with assaulting Private William Kerslake in the Atlantic Hotel six days earlier. The defendant pleaded not guilty and, after sworn evidence was given by Joseph Pender, John Thomas and PC Hill, the bench dismissed the case.

And so the war in 1915 progressed for Scilly, with the RNAPS drifters replaced by trawlers from 30 July, the CO's report saying:

'Now that the drifters have been taken away, I submit that the Mining Party, now consisting of one Torpedo Gunners Mate and twelve Special Ratings is superfluous and no longer

*required. If the TGM and his Mate were kept here to overhaul
and look after depth charges & keep the mining store in order,
they would be sufficient. One might be an armourer, to look
after the guns and rifles on the trawlers.'*

In August net mine stocks were reported as, *'Number returned to
Base 540; 96 condemned; exploded 8; lost 13; on boats 48, with 88
in the Mine Store.'* Between August and December the SS *Gamen*
was sunk, as was the Italian *Gem*, the SS *Swazi* and many others,
all of which received assistance from the base trawlers.

Taken up as a decoy ship in March 1915 and armed, the SS
Baralong, now *Q-2*, had not one encounter with a U-boat despite
having cruised around for some 12,000 miles until 19 August, when

Anti-submarine net mines, each carrying some 40lbs (18kg) of high
explosives. They are shown here laid out on a quay being inspected, before
loading onto an anti-submarine net-trawler, and were used extensively by the
RNAPS St Mary's. *(Imperial War Museum)*

A net-mine attached to a steel wire anti-submarine net being put over the side by a team of Royal Navy personnel. *(Imperial War Museum)*

she was between Queenstown (now Cobh in Ireland) and Scilly. Eight British ships had been sunk in the area including the White Star SS *Arabic*, so *Q-2*, disguised as an American cargo ship with US colours painted on wooden boards hung over each side, was sent into the area. *Q-2* then picked up a radio SOS message from the SS *Nicosan* carrying mules, and on reaching the location found six lifeboats full of men close to a U-boat which proved to be *U-27*, all hidden behind the sinking steamer.

Barralong pulled in the boards hanging overboard, changed the US flag for the white ensign and, hidden from view behind the damaged *Nicosan*, waited for the U-boat to emerge into the open. The moment it did they opened fire, caught the Germans totally unprepared and sank the submarine at a range of only 600 yards. Within five weeks *Barralong* had done it again, sinking *U-41* in much the same way south-west of the Bishop Rock. Her commanding officer, Lieutenant Commander Wilmot-Smith, was

RNAPS armed trawlers on trot moorings off Newman House, the Garrison. The steamship (top centre) is the famous Q-ship SS *Barralong*. *(Richard Larn Collection)*

awarded a DSO and Engineer Dowie a DSC. The Prize Court later awarded the ship's company £1,000 to be shared between them.

A strange entry in Anne Banfield's diary for 6 September, written at Alverton Vean, Penzance, where she lived, reads:

> *'Old Bruce, your spy, arrested on St Mary's last week, who was sent to the mainland this morning, was arrested last week and put under guard of two soldiers – one day, one night, followed him wherever he went. Rumour says he was caught showing lights on Kitty Down, just opposite Longstone. So whether he will be shot or not I can't tell. I hope so. Saw Lizzie off for Scilly on the Arimathea.'*

The background to this was that Annie and a friend Winifred were walking in the Argy Moor area, near Watermill on 7 July, when they saw a man whom they took to be a German spy and tracked but then lost him. On Sunday, 25 July they were walking in the Penninis area when they saw the man again, whom they decided must be a spy. They found out he was staying at Tregarthen's Hotel and reported the matter to the military.

In October the government's Derby scheme was enacted, whereby men aged 18 to 41 'attested' or 'agreed' to enlist when asked to do so. These men were issued with arm bands and an Attestation Card, the bands being khaki in colour with a scarlet crown to show their readiness to serve. These were in retaliation to the 'white feathers' being given to men of military age not in uniform on the mainland, but it is doubtful if the scheme had much effect on the islands.

The RNAPS suffered its first drifter loss on 13 November when No.1900 *Silvery Wave*, 96 tons, armed with a 6-pounder gun was wrecked whilst returning from a four-day patrol in company with the *Boy Eddie*. Caught in a gale, they sought shelter in Crow Sound but were driven into Water Mill Cove, near Pelistry Bay, where the *Silvery Wave* became a total loss. By the end of 1915 Great Britain had lost 430 ships to U-boats and the nation found itself with less than six weeks supply of wheat left.

CHAPTER 3

1916
The Western Approaches
become a killing ground

On 5 January the Military Service Act came into force, which made men between 18 and 40 years of age liable for call up. It was later extended to the age of 51. The Compulsion Bill which also came into effect announced that within five weeks all single young men for whom there was no excuse, would be in khaki, the 19 to 26 year olds having already been called up. Initially married men were exempt, but as the war progressed, even they were called up which caused great concern amongst the farming community of Scilly, who wondered who would work the land. The Act resulted in three Scillonians joining the army that month, with eleven local Royal Naval Reservists called up to serve.

Food shortages were now being felt on the mainland, but fortunately the Isles of Scilly were reasonably self-sufficient apart from sugar, tea, coffee, fruit and flour. On 29 January the President of the Board of Trade, Mr Rundsman, restricted the importation of paper-making materials, raw tobacco, building materials, furniture timber and some fruits; also the price of granulated sugar escalated.

Flour to make bread came from Penzance in 120lb (55kg) bags,

Four friends home on leave from the services (back row, L-R) Vivian Ellis; Alfred Lethbridge; (front) John Sherris; William Phillips. *(John & Kay Banfield)*

which in 1916 was still readily available. Until 1905 St Mary's had a communal bakery in Silver Street run by 'Baker' Nance, to whom islanders could take their dough and cakes for him to bake. When done, these were placed outside on a table with either a mark or limpet shells to identify their owner. Prior to the Silver Street bakery, Scillonians would have baked their own as people had for centuries, but then a Penzance company offered a delivery service and baskets of bread would be sent over from the mainland. Locals complained the loaves were expensive and it is surprising they could afford this service, especially since the bread took two or three days to arrive and was invariably stale on arrival.

After 'Baker' Nance died, a Mr Ashford took over but faced competition from Percy Chirgwin JP, who owned a general store on the Bank, one in Penzance and three more on the mainland, who obtained the lucrative contract to supply all the vessels attached to the naval base, the bread being sent over from Penzance. Chirgwin's then lost the contract following complaints that the loaves were always stale, so the local bakery stepped in again offering a much better service. Ashford's two helpers were his son Bertie, and Albert Pender, two 17 year olds, who got up at 3am to light the fire and prepare the dough. The two boys then delivered the loaves to the ships in a hand cart, but with the quay deeply rutted at the time, the cart frequently overset throwing the loaves into puddles and potholes, which they picked up wet and sometimes dirty, but delivered anyway! When visiting warships called in, some with crews in excess of 1,000, the volume of bread ordered from the bakery was prodigious and very profitable, requiring extra manpower.

As more and more ships were sunk off Scilly by U-boats, so the magistrates were kept busy with inquests on drowned seamen, in addition to local disturbances. On 16 January Arthur Lowther, a naval seaman aged 20-25, was charged with assaulting Albert Poynter, landlord of the Atlantic Hotel, St Mary's. The prisoner, who had been in custody since his arrest on 6 January, pleaded guilty and was ordered to pay a fine of 18s with 3s costs. On 4 March, Deputy Coroner Frederick Ward held an inquest into the death of 24-year-old Alexander Grant, second engineer from a steam drifter, whose body was found in St Mary's harbour. The jury of twelve viewed the body in the mortuary and then heard evidence from Private Charles Williams, a sentry on the quay, who saw the deceased step over the edge of the quay and disappear that night. Evidence was heard from John Toms, a deck boy belonging to the drifter, James Main, the skipper, Alexander Hutchinson first engineer and Royal Marine Sergeant R. Holmes. The verdict was that the deceased accidentally drowned after falling from St Mary's quay in the extreme darkness of the night of 3 March, the jury suggesting that the edge of the quay should be whitewashed. No mention was made during the hearing of the RNAPS drifter's name, presumably for security reasons.

When the council met on 29 April, it was proposed permission be granted to give accommodation in the Poor House on the Strand to John Pearce. "If he returns to Scilly on furlough, he being on active service at the front and likely to obtain leave to visit his mother, Mrs Taylor who runs the establishment."

Two months later Alfred Trenear of Buzza Street, St Mary's, a mason's labourer, was charged with having been enlisted under the Military Services Act, 1916, but *'without leave lawfully granted or such sickness or other reasonable excuse as may be allowed in the prescribed manner, failed to appear at the time and place at which he was required upon such calling out to attend.'* The defendant was ordered to pay £2 with a further 4s costs, to be deducted from his pay as a soldier, and after to be immediately taken into military custody and sent to the mainland.

There was grave concern in mid-June when the ferry, the SS *Lyonesse* broke free of her moorings alongside the quay in a severe gale, drifted right across the harbour and ended up beached high and dry under the windows of the Strand and Custom Houses. Fortunately she settled into the soft sandy foreshore suffering no damage and was refloated by tugs at high water none the worse for the accident. Also in June, the St Mary's Girl Guides gave a credible public display of their skills as signallers, using semaphore and the Morse code, witnessed by a large crowd on the Garrison. They had been practising for only two months under the guidance of their

St Mary's Girl Guides, 1915, outside the entrance to Star Castle. Like the boys in the CLB, Girl Guides were taught semaphore and Morse code and were used as messengers between the W/T station at Telegraph and the White House Naval HQ, or the Military HQ, at Star Castle. *(St Mary's Museum)*

instructor, Lance Corporal Hale, Royal Marines, who was assisted by Mrs Walker and Miss Hill.

Letters sent home from the Western Front by soldiers were subject to censure, therefore seldom contained any graphic details as to what life was really like in the trenches. One exception was an article passed to the *Royal Cornwall Gazette* (RCG) by a private in the Devon and Cornwall Light Infantry, believed to be George Payne, who came from Scilly but moved to Truro where he was a member of the RCG's printing staff. He probably wrote this piece for the newspaper whilst on leave, or else somehow smuggled it to his previous employer's office.

'When a battalion are for duty in the trenches they come from their rest billets, which are usually 3-4 miles from the firing line, and take up a position in the supports (trenches), spending the day in dugouts, and at 7.30pm parade to draw rations, brought to the Brigade by transports. The distance we had to go was about 2.5 miles each way. We fall in in single file and march off, but we do not follow the road as it is targeted by enemy guns, so we find our own way across fields and woods and keep close to the hedges as far as we can, and in the dark, through mud and water and slippery paths, it is a rough journey. We get to HQ and each man gets his share (of ammunition or equipment) to carry. We then march back and think ourselves very fortunate as all the time we are under fire and shells are bursting and bullets are whizzing around. As the bullets whistle over, each man ducks his head, the night lights are going up and we halt as our movements would be seen to bring a hail of bullets. On we*

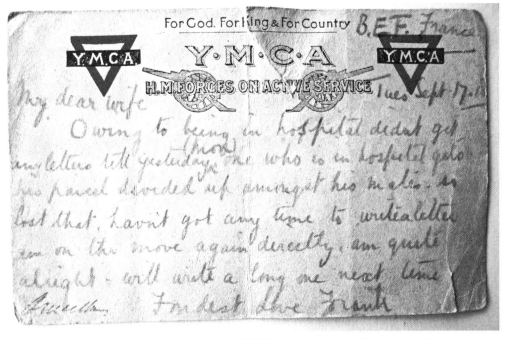

Poignant postcard home from the BEF in France, dated September 1917, stating that the writer, Frank Pender, 'owing to being in hospital didn't get your letters till yesterday'. (John & Kay Banfield)

The Lethbridge family, who lived in Thoroughfare, St Mary's, and had six sons in the armed forces; back row L-R, James, George, William, Matthew; middle row, Mary, James, Kathleen. Front row, John and Alfred. They all survived WWI. (John & Kay Banfield)

go, a word is passed back "mind the shell hole on the right", or "there's a fallen tree across the road or path". A word from our officer, "man hit". My first night on supply our sergeant was shot through the leg. We get back to our supports, taking six hours to cover the five miles. We fall down and are soon asleep. We never remove our boots or clothes; always sleep in full equipment and ammunition, our rifle by our side.

We are roused at 8am and each man given his rations for the day. If we can find a stream we wash, but have to be careful we are not seen. We can't have hot tea, no fires are allowed, so we just add cold water from derelict farm house wells. I spent four days on what we call supports; we then went to reserve trenches near the front line, arriving at midnight. It was fearful, raining and very dark and mud in the trenches up to our knees. Got news that one of my comrades had been shot through the head. He foolishly looked over the parapet to see if there were any Germans about, and a sniper shot him. I saw him buried in the wood ten minutes later. Another chap took his coat off to have a wash, when a whiz-bang exploding bullet hit his elbow, shattering his arm. I was standing close to him; the stretcher bearers soon took him away to the ambulance car and on to a field hospital.

At night we either fetched rations or carried bricks for the sappers. We get the bricks from the shattered houses. Next night I took my place in the firing line, a German trench only 50 yards in front of me. My mate's rifle was hit by a bullet which knocked him off the parapet into the trench and two foot of mud which was freezing.'

During the early months of 1916 U-boats continued to sink merchantmen off Scilly, the 2,007 ton SS *Rothesay* 30 miles southwest of the Bishop Rock on 5 March and the French barquentine *Sainte Marie* on 7 April. Then on 18 May the 276 ton armed trawler *Carbineer*, one of the St Mary's RNAPS fleet, was wrecked in dense fog on Crebawethan, out in the Western Rocks, her crew saved by the drifter *John S. Summers*. A Royal Navy salvage party was sent out from St Mary's, but found her hull so badly holed nothing could be done, so they set about recovering stores and her gun. A Lloyd's salvage officer arrived on 19 May and, accompanied by Lieutenant Thompson RNR, went out to the Western Rocks but as the wreck had already broken in two they decided not to board her. The

The torpedoed SS.*Gaasterland* and the armed trawlers *Foss* and *City of Edinburgh* off Scilly which went out to save her. *(St Mary's Museum)*

Lloyd's man wrote her off, declaring the *'salvage of the vessel quite impossible; no salvage company would undertake it on a no-cure no-pay basis'*.

The weekly reports to the Vice Admiral, Falmouth, of events happening at the St Mary's RNAPS sub-station, make for interesting but repetitive reading.

6 June 1916 – No.2664 *Dewland* and 1579 *Emerald* watering. Captain-in-Charge (C-in-C), Falmouth arrived and inspected the Base. No.1191 *Whitefriars* returned to port with defective WT (Wireless Telegraphy) transformer; part landed and ship returned to patrol.

9 June – Unit 92 proceeded on patrol (a unit consisted of three ships), Unit 85 returned to port, No.1361 *Hercules* and 1359 *City of Edinburgh* watering, the latter alongside for engine repairs and fitting of a minesweeping gantry. No coaling done this day, as all vessels now coaled to fullest capacity. Commander Oliver RN at sea inspecting drifters. List attached of all seventeen vessels that have completed 24 hours at sea for four or five days.

10 June – Total number of mines received on St Mary's Station now 700; condemned, 3; exploded, 8; lost, 13; remaining on boats 252; in store here, 88. No.1359 *City of Edinburgh* in the Pool for engineering purposes, No.1358 *Cambria* at the pier taking in stores for survey at Devonport; No.1376 *Diamond* arrived back from refit, now fitting mine-sweeping gantry. [Author's Note: The mines to which this report refers were not large oval moored mines fitted with contact horns laid in fields, but smaller cylindrical mines attached to steel drift nets slung between two vessels in the hope a submarine might become entangled. These 'net mines' as they were called, could then be fired electrically from the parent vessel, hopefully causing an entangled U-boat to sink.]

Group photograph of some 94 Royal Navy staff of RNAPS *St Mary's* c1916, taken in Buzza Quarry, showing naval officers, warrant officers, ratings, Royal Marines, WRNS, and one female not in uniform. *(St Mary's Museum)*

30 June – List of all twenty naval vessels currently based at St Mary's and their armament; No.1192 *St Ives* (minesweeper, 3pdr gun); No.2659 *Kőnig Frederick III* (12pdr gun); No.1361 *Hercules IV* (minesweeper, 3pdr gun); No.1358 *Cambria* (3pdr gun); No.1359 *City of Edinburgh*; (3pdr gun); No.1191 *Whitefriars* (3pdr gun); No.1376 (3pdr gun); *Diamond* (no gun); No.1579 *Emerald* (12pdr gun); No.1757 *Ottili* (3pdr gun); No.2664 *Dewaland* (12pdr gun); No.2662 *Hatano* (3pdr gun); No.1380 *Anthony Hope* (3pdr gun); No.1195 *Semno* (3pdr gun); No.1179 *Loch Navero* (3pdr gun); No.1185 *Sophes* (3pdr gun); No.963 *Newbridge* (3pdr gun); No.1759 *Merrydale* (3pdr gun); No.1180 *Andrew Marvel* (3pdr gun); No.1182 *Strathelliot*; (6pdr gun); No.1360 *Nancy Hague* (3pdr gun).

In August the council agreed that Relief in Kind to the amount of 5s should be granted to the wife and family of Stephen Pender, seaman, and that their grocery account be paid, and if not repaid application be made to the steamer on which Pender was serving. It was later reported that on 30 September 2s 6d had been recovered from Mrs Pender and she had promised to repay the balance during the coming week. Mrs Pender had eight children and had had relief of 4s twice. That week she was given food to the value of 10s since no steamer had arrived with the mail, therefore she had not received the allotment money she expected.

There were now so many servicemen and women on St Mary's, Army, Royal Navy, Royal Marines and WRNS, that the Church Hall was opened as an Army and Navy Club, where various entertainments and non-alcoholic drinks were provided. C.J. King, who ran the chemist's shop on the Bank and was one of the islands' photographers, announced a reduction in the charge he made for his weekly 'Picture Show' in the hall, asking the church committee to be allowed to use the front entrance *'so that those attending did not run all over the hall'*.

By June 1916 RNAS Mullion, situated on 320 acres of high ground belonging to the Bonython estate, near the village of Cury, north-east of Mullion, Cornwall, was in operation. Known as the

A group of some 100 servicemen and civilians outside Chirgwin's shop, at the Bank, St Mary's, probably awaiting the arrival of the *Lyonesse* ferry to take them to Penzance. Some of the soldiers are wearing full military packs and have probably been at home on leave or else convalescence. *(St Mary's Museum, Isles of Scilly)*

Lizard Airship Station, it operated from two huge hangars, the largest measuring 358ft in length, its doors when open offering 110ft clear width and 75ft height. These could accommodate two Coastal Class C9 airships and two smaller ones. Meantime, work began on the construction of another RNAS base in late 1916, this one at Newlyn, close to the south harbour, which employed Short 184 floatplanes. Once RNAS Tresco had become established, these came under the umbrella of RNAS South Western Group, whose headquarters were at Mount Wise, Devonport. These airships and floatplanes were of great assistance to the Isles of Scilly, offering air cover for merchant ships still sailing alone and helping to suppress U-boat activities. Unfortunately, the first attempt to establish a Royal Naval Air Station on the Isles of Scilly in 1917 went disastrously wrong.

Until now the RNAPS trawlers and drifters when not on patrol, either moored out on the 'trot', alongside the quay or else anchored

A Royal Naval Air Service C9 Coastal Class airship flying over the Isles of Scilly in 1917. *(Richard Larn Collection)*

in the Pool, the latter being hazardous in bad weather. The Base weekly report for 17 August tells us that the Royal Navy mooring vessel *Volunteer* had arrived under escort, with buoys and chain to lay a series of trot moorings in the Roads, to which patrol vessels could tie up at night in safety with their crews aboard.

Inevitably, some of the Scillonians who had gone to war were killed or wounded. Early in 1916 news was received that Petty Officer William Woodcock had been lost when HMS *Monmouth* was sunk, his name not having been included in the original list of five men from the islands killed on board. Sergeant George Harrison, 1st Grenadier Guards was killed in action on 25 September; Corporal W. Nicholls, Middlesex Regiment was killed in action in November, whilst Fred Steel, Royal Engineers, was badly gassed. Others who died were Chief Petty Officer Albert Delves, 26 September; Private Geoffrey Addison, 5th Battalion, 1st

Canadian Division, 26 September; Arthur Webber, Devon and Cornwall Light Infantry; Private Millman, also DCLI; William Tatham RN, who died at Plymouth in December, whilst the brothers Privates Arnold and Allan Nance were reported as wounded in November, the latter seriously but now in hospital.

The islands' magistrates met, unusually, at Holgate's Hotel on 2 September 1916, to resolve a most unusual case, in which Egbert Nicholas Mumford of St Mary's, hotel keeper, was charged by Commander William Oliver RN, that on or about 8 September 1916 he did spread a false report thereby contravening the regulations made under the Defence of the Realm Acts 1914 and 1915. Evidence on oath was taken of Lieutenant Bryce Thomson RNR, Skipper Arthur Kemp RNR, Skipper Edgar Garnham RNR and fisherman Ernest Guy. The defendant pleaded not guilty and gave evidence on oath in his defence. The accused was convicted as charged, ordered to pay a fine of £1, including costs, which suggests the offence was minor, but no details were released on security grounds.

Unidentified Private soldier from St Martin's, believed to have been related to the Bond family. *(Keith Low, St Martin's)*

On 1 July, General Sir Douglas Haig, commander-in-chief of the BEF launched his Somme offensive. On that day alone there were almost 58,000 casualties of whom 19,240 lost their lives. It remains the worst day in the history of the British Army.

A significant invention by the British, the military tank, which was first deployed in action on 15 September during the Battle of the Somme, made a significant impact on trench warfare. The Mk.1 version, equipped with two 6pdr guns and three machine guns was called either 'Mother', the 'Trench Dreadnought', or simply the 'Tin Box' by our soldiers, the Germans initially giving it the name *Shützengrabenvernichtungspanzerkraftwagen*.

The closing months of 1916 on Scilly saw much RNAPS activity, starting with trawler No 1191 *Whitefriars* on 28 November. Whilst on patrol off Scilly she intercepted a radio SOS signal from the SS *Swazi*, 5,000 tons, London registered, reporting she was being shelled by a submarine, 15 miles south of the Bishop Rock. The trawler asked the *Swazi* if she could steer for Scilly, only to be told that the submarine lay in that direction blocking her escape. The trawler's skipper then radioed *'We are closing in on you from all sides'*, which the U-boat must have intercepted since the shelling stopped immediately and the submarine submerged. As *Whitefriars* got closer to the *Swazi*'s position, she came across the Spanish registered SS *Santa Eugenia*, originally named *Ely Rise*, which actually had a German submarine alongside which immediately made off, the trawler's 3-pounder gun unfortunately having insufficient range to attack the U-boat.

The RNAPS report to Falmouth five days later included a statement by Lieutenant Armstrong RN, commanding officer of HMS *Q-9*, one of the new decoy vessels, a three-masted steel schooner whose real name was SV *Mary M. Mitchell* owned by Lord Penryn. Whilst in Falmouth loading china-clay in April 1916, the Admiralty requisitioned her for war service. Now armed with one 12-pounder and two 6-pounder guns hidden inside false deck structures and with an all Royal Navy crew, she was operating in the waters around Scilly. She was under full sail when *Q-9* sighted a submarine on the surface only two miles ahead, then a second U-boat close to two lifeboats holding the crew of a Norwegian steamer recently sunk. The nearest U-boat submerged but the other commenced to shell the decoy ship, which dropped her guise and fired nine shells back, two of which hit the enemy vessel. It then submerged and fired a torpedo at *Q-9* which fortunately missed. When HM Trawler *Rosetta* arrived in support *Q-9* departed for St Mary's to make her report.

No less than thirty-four merchant ships were sunk off Scilly between 7 September and 17 December 1916, consisting of British, Dutch, Greek, Spanish, Norwegian, Italian, French and Swedish

Unidentified steamship that had been torpedoed off Scilly, with two armed trawlers from the RNAPS St Mary's in attendance, and an anti-submarine patrol airship overhead. *(Penlee House Gallery & Museum, Percy Sharp Collection)*

vessels, the smallest being the French SV *Mysotis* of 64 tons, the largest the Dutch SS *Antwerpen* of 7,953 tons.

Unfortunately, local casualties escalated with news that Private Thomas Ashford had been killed in action whilst serving with the Royal New Zealand Engineers on 2 July and Private George Herbert who was killed on 25 September. The Nance brothers, Arnold and Allan, both wounded, were still in hospital, also Private Thomas Phillips, whilst William Tatham RN, died in the Naval Hospital, Plymouth in December. Some of these men died during the Battle of the Somme, which started in July and ended in November, and resulted in a combined total of more than a million casualties for Britain and her empire forces, France and Germany.

One of the secret anti-submarine vessels patrolled the waters around Scilly was the sailing brigantine *Q-9*, the *Mary M. Mitchell.* This photograph shows her in company with an armed Motor Launch probably from Newlyn. *(Penlee House Gallery & Museum, Percy Sharp Collection)*

That November the number of clergy on Scilly was decreased from four to three. The church authorities concerned at the shortage, felt that to have four clergymen for a population of 2,000 was no longer justified, which meant that the Reverend W. Fookes would be leaving St Martin's before Christmas without replacement.

CHAPTER 4

1917

The islands become a major naval base

Over the first two months of 1917 two working parties known as Wyndemere and Felixstowe arrived on St Mary's, including members of the Royal Naval Air Service No.1 Construction Section. After clearing an area of sand dunes overlooking Porthmellon beach they erected a wooden aircraft hangar, followed by a concrete slipway through the dunes and across the beach. On 18 February two American Curtis H-12 flying boats arrived from Felixstowe, the first (No.8654) crewed by Flight Lieutenant McGill RN, Flight Sub Lieutenant Johnson RN and Leading Air Mechanic J. Lawrence, the second (No.8644) by Flight Lieutenant Railton RN, Flight Sub Lieutenant Whigham RN and Leading Air Mechanic J. Birse. These were not the first RNAS aircraft sent to Scilly. In 1916 a small number of Short 184 floatplanes had been posted to the islands, but having no shore base they had to be moored out in St Mary's Roads where they received considerable damage in bad weather and were withdrawn. However, as shipping losses around Scilly continued to escalate, the Admiralty decided to concentrate on the construction of RNAS Porthmellon. Over the period 25–28 February, two more

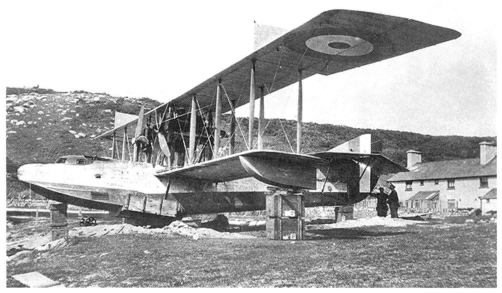

H-12 twin-engine seaplane No. 8654 on the foreshore at Tresco in February 1916 in front of Palace Row cottages, before the air station was built. *(St Mary's Museum)*

H-12 flying boats arrived, bringing with them Commander Hope-Vere RN, the station's new commanding officer, who made the first operational flight from Scilly against submarines, carrying two 65lb bombs in No.8656, on the actual day of his arrival.

Facing the prevailing westerly winds, RNAS Porthmellon frequently proved untenable regarding aircraft taking off, landing and recovery, and it was Flight Commander R. Maycock who suggested the base be moved to Tresco. An area of some 20 acres of waterfront south of New Grimsby harbour was acquired by the Admiralty from the Tresco Estate. Building commenced on what was to become the huge, highly successful, Royal Naval Air Station, Tresco. The construction crews lived under canvas in army bell tents erected on a flat area to the south designated for accommodation huts, but unable to survive the frequent gales. The temporary living area, including tents, wash houses, kitchens, stores etc. was moved to Simpson's Field, a sheltered area between the Great Pool and the Avenue. The flying boats were safely moored in Tresco Channel.

The Porthmellon site was then abandoned and slowly RNAS Tresco took shape until it eventually occupied 30 acres. Drifters and trawlers attached to the RNAPS returning from refit and repairs in Penzance brought with them huge quantities of cement in one-ton bags, whilst RN auxiliary ships brought the timber, steel and other building materials. Once a small Bessonneau hangar had been erected, along with stores and offices, work commenced on permanent barrack-type living blocks, the concrete bases of which can be seen to this day.

During those early days, aircrews and maintainers were billeted on St Mary's in Ennor House, Old Town, being ferried to and from St Mary's quay on a daily basis in the four solid-tyre lorries supplied for Porthmellon. Locals claim that these were the first ever motor

The original tented accommodation on Tresco for the men of No.1 Construction Section who were building RNAS Tresco. *(St Mary's Museum)*

An aerial view of RNAS Tresco under construction in its early days, with only the framework for a small steel hangar and one hut still being built; one seaplane sits on Grimsby Beach, a second on the wooden slipway. The black lump on the beach between the seaplanes is the remains of the shipwreck *Sophie. (St Mary's Museum, Isles of Scilly)*

Aerial view of the air station before the hangar was built, showing the accommodation blocks. *(St Mary's Museum, Isles of Scilly)*

vehicles on St Mary's and that two were later sold to Holgate's Hotel. Initially, there were some 400 naval personnel on Tresco, which grew to 700 and eventually to over 1,000 servicemen and women.

The original small Bessonneau hangar was then replaced with two larger wooden hangars, each of which could accommodate two H-12 seaplanes with their wings folded back. Later, these wooden hangars were replaced with a huge steel hangar to accommodate the F-2As and F-3 larger twin-engine seaplanes, whose wings could not easily be removed. Working together, the RNAPS and RNAS Tresco continued their daily but independent tasks of anti-submarine patrols, convoy escorts and generally protecting shipping in the Western Approaches to great effect, making a major contribution to the war at sea.

That January, the operating costs of the *Lyonesse* ferry were raised yet again in the Council of the Isles of Scilly, which was told that unless further financial help be given, the West Cornwall SS. Co. Ltd. could not possibly continue after June. In March negotiations between the Admiralty and the operating company came to a satisfactory agreement, so that neither the Dorrien-Smith family nor the council would be called on for higher pecuniary support. In amongst such serious matters as the ferry service, a petition was read *'requesting that the Town Hall might be let for dances by responsible persons'*. It was also requested that the Army Medical Board have free use of the Town Hall and rooms for medical inspection of the men of military age on the islands, both requests being approved.

Although St Mary's no longer had a kite balloon service station, in March 1917 two British destroyers entered the Roads deploying kite balloons whilst under way. The use of kite balloons by warships was nothing new, but this was the first time they had been seen deployed at sea around Scilly. Experiments were carried out over a period of four weeks around the islands, before the destroyers left for Plymouth.

The trawlers and drifters of the patrol service were particularly busy during the first two months of 1917, called out to assist seventeen steamships attacked and sunk by U-boats in addition to their usual anti-submarine patrols, rescue of survivors, mine sweeping, vessel examination, escorts and the laying of mine nets. The first call was to the Norwegian SS *Ellik*, 602 tons, torpedoed 40 miles south-west of the Bishop Rock on 2 January and then to the SS *Bestik* the same day, another larger Norwegian vessel, sunk by the same U-boat. The following day the French three-masted schooner *Aimee Marie* of 327 tons was stopped and explosive scuttling charges placed below decks. On 4 January the Russian sailing vessel *Ruby*, 949 tons, was sunk by submarine gunfire off Scilly. Two more ships were sent to the bottom before the end of the month, the Norwegian SS *Asp* and SS *Hekla*, the former sunk by shellfire, the latter torpedoed. During the first three weeks of February, *U-53* sank two ships, the SS *Housatonic*, 3,143 tons carrying wheat, and the French schooner *Marthe* carrying salt. Ironically, the *Housatonic*, whilst registered in New Orleans and flying the American flag, was an ex-German vessel named *Pickhuben*, which had been interned at the outbreak of the war, then sold to an American owner. Crew from the U-boat went aboard and opened her seacocks, but she took so long to sink a torpedo was used to finish her off.

On 4 February the submarine *UC-47* sank the Dunkirk schooner *Marthe* using explosive charges and the American SS *Japanese Prince*, 4876 tons, using a single torpedo, taking advantage of the German announcement that from 1 February the policy of unrestricted submarine warfare would be resumed. This may well have been the last straw for the Americans since on 6 April they declared war on Germany.

On 16 February Scilly experienced its worst maritime disaster when *U-21* put paid to a convoy of eight neutral Dutch ships, sinking six of them in one day. According to 'official sources', the Dutch ships left Amsterdam for the United States putting into Falmouth on passage. On the morning of 21 February, they sailed for the Western Approaches, their destination New York and

Philadelphia. It was a beautiful sunny day without a breath of wind, the surface of the sea like a mill pond when, some 30 miles north-west of the Bishop Rock three of the ships were torpedoed in a matter of minutes. Three others had scuttling charges placed on board, whilst two managed to escape, one being the SS *Menado*, which was towed back to Falmouth by a trawler. The combined crews of the six ships, since no lives were lost, filled twenty-eight boats, and made a spectacular entry into St Mary's led by the St Agnes lifeboat *Charles Deere James*.

That was the account generally believed and published many times over until Tony Pawlyn, the librarian at the National Maritime Museum, Falmouth, looked deeper into the event and a different story emerged. Eight independent Dutch ships were stopped in the Channel by British warships between October and January and ordered into Falmouth for examination of their cargo in case they were carrying contraband. Once cleared, the authorities refused them permission to sail, on the grounds they were liable to be sunk, so they remained in Falmouth Roads at anchor. The Dutch government then applied to Germany for immunity from attack and a letter was eventually received granting them safe passage. Hence, they sailed together but not as a convoy, since some of them wanted to get to Dutch ports, others to the United States. The letter of 'safe passage' was seemingly never communicated to the commanding officer of *U-21*, who saw the eight ships as legitimate targets on 22 February and set about sinking them all! The six sunk were the SS *Bandoeng*, SS *Eemlan*, SS *Gaasterland*, SS *Jacatr*, SS *Noorderdijk* and the SS *Zaandijk*, and somewhere amongst these the Norwegian SS *Normanna* became mixed up with the encounter, *U-21* sinking her with explosive charges. Another intriguing aspect of this story, supported by photographs, is that the Dutch ships were painted with 'dazzle camouflage' whilst in Falmouth, the ship's names being superimposed in large letters on both sides of each vessel.

What on earth were neutral Dutch ships doing being given this special treatment to make them difficult for submarines to attack? We may never know. The Netherlands Section of the League of

A RN gun-boat painted in dazzle camouflage. This was believed to break up the outline of a ship, making it difficult for a U-boat to aim a torpedo accurately. *(Penlee Gallery, Short collection)*

A Curtiss H-12 seaplane moored off air station at RNAS Tresco in Channel. *(St Mary's Museum)*

Neutral Countries awarded a special medal to each lifeboat crew member, as well as the crews of RNAPS trawlers involved in the rescue, presented by Mrs Dorrien-Smith on St Mary's. With over 500 survivors landed on the quay at St Mary's, armed guards were posted to contain them, and the following day Edward McDonald, the St Mary's Mission to Seamen agent, was busy distributing clothing on the wide pavement opposite the Bishop and Wolf Inn, to those men still scantily dressed before they were sent to Penzance on board the *Lyonesse*.

An inquest held on St Martin's on 13 March, concerned an unidentified body found in the sea near Treweek's Island the previous day. The body was viewed and evidence heard from Douglas Skinner who found the body, Nicholas Christopher, John Goddard and Joseph Hicks, who brought the body to Higher Town in their boat, where it was landed. A search of the body found a gold chain fastened to the waistcoat with a watch attached inscribed 'Peter Peterson, Pilestrœde 3, Kjobenhavn' (watch no: 5/333-24), also a lifebuoy encircling the body marked 'Lars Kruse – Kobenhavn'. A verdict was given that the said person, apparently Danish, a male, found in the sea, aged 50-60, had died from drowning. With no police presence on St Martin's, it was decided not to waste the time of Sergeant William Hill nor his eight constables on St Mary's, nor the constables on Tresco, St Agnes and Bryher in attending the inquest.

The continued sinking of American ships had led President Woodrow Wilson to declare war on Germany in April, but Congress did not pass a Selective Service Act until May. It was June before the 1st US Infantry Division arrived in France to support the Allied troops at the front.

The *Cornishman* newspaper of 22 March 1917, reported on the sitting of the Cornwall War Tribunal in Truro which was contesting the conditional military exemption granted to M. Mumford, a married butcher living on St Mary's. The military, which appealed, contended that the man was not in a certified occupation and his partner, aged 37, had also been exempted. The applicant, who was not present, had written to the tribunal saying that if he was taken his partner would be the only butcher there. Should the partner become ill, there would be meatless days on the island with a vengeance. Mr David Howell said they were not asking to have the exemption of the partner reviewed and the military appeal was allowed. Another case the same day concerned S.N. Trenear, single, aged 19, a carpenter on the Isles of Scilly. He had been exempted until May 15 locally and the military were objecting. He too lost his case and had to sign up.

By now RNAS Tresco was making daily anti-submarine patrols and on 27 April FB8654 had a lucky escape when she engaged a U-boat on the surface. The enemy returned fire and the flying boat was forced to return to base when her propeller was hit and damaged by machine-gun bullets. May 1917 was a particularly busy month, the station losing FB8664 on 9 May when it crashed either off St Agnes, Gugh or Peninnis Head, killing Flight Lieutenant Railton, Flight Sub Lieutenant Wigham and, on May 27, Leading Mechanic Birse.

On at least two occasions bombs aimed at submarines, having failed to release due to severe salt water corrosion of the Bowden cable-operated mechanism, fell off seaplanes on landing, on one occasion destroying the aircraft and killing two men. This problem was resolved by Chief Petty Officer Artificer Tadman over a few evenings whilst in his lodgings with Mrs Frances Watts on the Parade, St Mary's. Producing a drawing of a new release mechanism, CPO Tadman got a local blacksmith to make up some steel parts for him which were finished off by hand in a Tresco workshop. The completely new bomb release mechanism was submitted to the station's commanding officer for approval. The new device proved an immediate success and was fitted to all the aircraft. Incidentally, CPO Tadman returned to Scilly in 1919 and married Mrs Watt's niece, Annie, the couple settling in Broadstairs, Kent.

Until the new accommodation blocks on Tresco were completed, all the aircrew and maintainers continued to be billeted on St Mary's. At dawn boats left St Mary's quay every day with mechanics and armourers who would prepare the aircraft required

Seaplanes on the hard-standing in front of the large hangar on Tresco.
(St Mary's Museum, Isles of Scilly)

that day. The bombs were ferried out to the aircraft in dinghies
where an armourer, lying flat on his back, cradled a small bomb on
his stomach whilst it was fitted to the aircraft's release mechanism.
One morning, 6 June, some men were walking across the dunes
towards the old potato store which was now the bomb store, after
landing at New Grimsby, when they saw an armourer trying to fuse
a bomb. The fuse he inserted in the nose proved to be stiff, so he
began to hit it with a piece of wood. Aware what might follow they
flung themselves to the ground, which was just as well, since the
bomb exploded, causing the bomb store to be completely destroyed.

The armourer responsible, Aircraftsman Second Class Charles
Ellingsworth of Ramsgate, aged 20, was blown to pieces, a petty
officer lost an eye, another aircraftsman named William Creasy was
badly injured and later died. Both Ellingsworth and Creasy are
buried in the same grave in Tresco churchyard, but there seems to
be some confusion, since Creasy, according to the grave inscription,
died on 31 May.

As one would expect of an air station of such a size, there were
many accidents to aircraft. It was 11 March when H-12 No.8652
had to be beached at Newlyn when it started to sink out in Mount's

Three armourers displaying the three types of bombs the H-12 aircraft carried on anti-submarine patrols. The weapon on the right is a 112lb High Explosive, Laboratories Mk.3 bomb (HE.RL). *(St Mary's Museum, Isles of Scilly)*

The remains of the bomb store, known as the old 'Bothy', following the detonation of a bomb which killed two armourers and injured a third. *(St Mary's Museum, Isles of Scilly)*

Bay, and on 5 June H-12 No.8654 landed on the sea off Trevose Head, North Cornwall during a patrol. It proved difficult, but was successfully recovered.

The feared telegram concerning the death of Private 12988 Alfred George Phillips, 1st Battalion Devon and Cornwall Light Infantry, reached the home of his parents, John Honey Phillips and stepmother Sarah Ann Phillips of Anglesea House, the Strand, St Mary's, only four days after a letter had been received from him

RNAS Tresco showing the completed hangar, some huts and a wooden slipway used to launch and recover seaplanes. *(Mike Harcum Collection)*

dated 4 May 1917. Addressed to his sister, it reads as follows, verbatim, including spelling errors:

'Dear Siss, a few lines in answer to your most welcome letter glad to see that you are all quite well. I am in the pink myself but we are having a very hard time out here but it is lovely fine weather most to hot sometimes but we are giving the Germans something to go on with. Well you said that you had

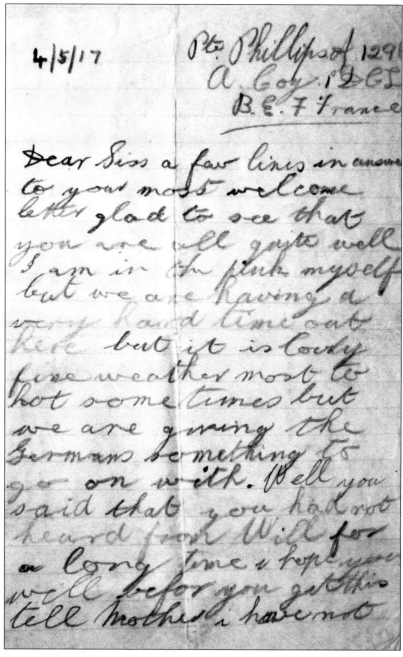

4/5/17

Pte Phillips of 129.
A. Coy 1 DCLI
B.E.F France

Dear Siss a few lines in answer to your most welcome letter glad to see that you are all quite well I am in the pink myself but we are having a very hard time out here but it is lovely fine weather most too hot some times but we are giving the Germans something to go on with. Well you said that you had not heard from Will for a long time i hope you will before you get this tell Mother i have not

Letter from Private Alfred Phillips, A. Company 1, DCLI, to his sister on St Mary's. Born at Penninnis View, Old Town, St Mary's, his family moved to Anglesea House, the Strand. He has no known grave having been killed on the battlefield 8 May 1917, but is commemorated at the Arras Memorial, Pas de Calais, France. Bay 7. *(John & Kay Banfield) not heard from Will for a long time and hope you will before you get this. Tell mother i have not had her parcle yet but i am looking forward for it, tell her i should like about a dozen pasties and two or three caks for we don't get over fed out here now sometimes we are two or three days without getting a bit to eat. Well, tell Mother i will write her and Father soon, now i will close as there is no more news i will write again soon now, ta ta from your loving brother, Alfred. X X X X X X'*

Alfred was killed in action on 8 May 1917, aged 26. He has no known grave but is commemorated on the Arras Memorial in the Pas de Calais, France, Bay 7. The family later heard from William, Alfred's brother, that the two had met up by accident in the trenches the night before they both went 'over the top' into battle. William asked Alfred if he would transfer to his unit but he refused, saying he thought he should stay with his comrades.

On the home front, all councils, including the Isles of Scilly were instructed to appoint a War Agricultural Committee, to look after the growing of food and ensure that farms were being used to their best advantage. This meant sacrificing land previously given over to flower farming to growing vegetables, which was not popular, but with little or no market for flowers on the mainland, vegetables earned an income and helped the war effort. Since certain foodstuffs were now becoming scarce, food rationing was being considered.

The RNAPS were advised on 10 May that the Admiralty was to introduce convoys for vessels crossing the Atlantic, each having Royal Navy escorts. This meant that St Mary's trawlers and drifters had to escort fewer individual ships other than convoy stragglers, allowing both them and the RNAS to concentrate on finding and destroying submarines. This they did on 24 May, when H-12, a Curtis Large Americas seaplane, No 8656 took off in response to a report of a surfaced submarine. Fifteen minutes later it was spotted on their starboard bow, and they turned to attack, dropping four 100lb bombs, scoring direct hits forward of the submarine's conning tower. The submarine was seen to sink by the bow, her stern coming out of the water at an angle of 60 degrees. The crew of the H-12 observed

The Royal Navy armed motor launch ML-363 at sea on anti-submarine patrol. These carried depth charges from 1916 onwards. *(Penlee House Gallery & Museum, Percy Sharp Collection)*

bubbles, foam and a considerable quantity of surface oil before turning back for Tresco. On their initial approach the submarine opened fire with machine guns, a bullet hitting the starboard engine radiator causing a serious leak. Crewman Chief Petty Officer Engineer Tadman climbed out onto the wing and plugged the bullet hole with his handkerchief, remaining there holding it in place until the aircraft landed back at base. Flight Lieutenants Hoare and Anderson, pilot and co-pilot, received DSCs, Chief Petty Officer Tadman a CGM and wireless operator Roy Chapman a DSM. On inspection the aircraft was found to have been hit eight times. Flight Lieutenant Anderson, the co-pilot and a very sensitive man, became very depressed over the death of the submarine's crew, taking holy orders after the war and eventually became the Bishop of Salisbury.

The submarine was the *UC-66*, a mine-layer) which carried a crew of 23, none of whom survived. Her captain, Oberleutnant Herbert Pustkuchen, in charge of *UC-66* for five patrols, had already sunk 32 ships and damaged six others, representing 44,506-tons. This incident was the only German U-boat sunk by an aircraft in the First World War, and William Anderson one of only a few men who could claim to have served in the army, the navy (RNAS) and the Royal Air Force, his final posting being chaplain at the Britannia Royal Navy College. Three days later the same aircraft but with a different crew, dropped two 100lb bombs on a submarine, both of which detonated forward of the conning tower, and like *UC-66* her stern came at a steep angle, but despite a large oil slick over the site she appears to have survived, since German U-Boat records do not report another boat missing for that period. On 23 July two colliers arrived, the SS *Artificer* and the SS *A.B. Sherman*, and a working party commenced to discharge them immediately. Five days later Land's End passed on a message from Mullion RNAS at 1600 that one of their airships was dropping bombs on a suspected submarine in 49° 43′N; 06° 30′W, and No.1191 *Whitefriars* and No.1360 *Nancy Hague* were sent to investigate, but nothing was found.

A red letter day for the RNAPS was 30 July 1917 when an advanced form of underwater technology was trialled in Scilly, that would greatly assist them to detect the presence of German U-boats whilst submerged. Trawler No.1191 *Whitefriars* went out with Commander Oliver RN and Lieutenant Smith RN to experiment with Mk II Directional Hydrophones, using HM Motor Launch *ML319* from Newlyn which was towing an 'underwater target', presumably some sort of device which simulated U-boat propeller noises. They remained at sea all day making long and short distance 'runs' from every angle on the target before returning to St Mary's. The experiments had proved more than satisfactory. This was the forerunner of passive sonar, initially a simple listening device tuned to pick up propeller noises, which after the war was slowly developed to be fitted to both ships and submarines to become both passive (listening) and active (transmitting) sonar as we know it today.

An intercepted radio message on 31 July from the French tug SS *Bramley*, 215 tons, stated, 'SOS – sinking fast by the head 49° 30′N, 06° 46′W send two tugs'. The tugs *Joseph Constantine* and *Atlanta III* as well as the trawlers *Foss, City of Edinburgh* and the drifter *Marvellous* went out past the Bishop Rock where they were joined by a Newlyn-based motor launch and seaplanes. HM destroyer *Hardy*, which was in the vicinity responded by radio, 'Rescue tug will stand by', whilst trawlers *Bramley Rose* and No.3278 *Foss*

Anti-submarine listening hydrophone trials conducted from a drifter. Note the hydrophone about to be lowered into the sea, and four Royal Navy personnel wearing listening headphones. *(Imperial War Museum)*

Gun crew on board a Royal Navy armed motor launch exercising their 12-pounder deck gun. *(Penlee House Gallery & Museum, Percy Sharp Collection)*

reported: 'Am about to pick up casualty, 10 miles from Bishop, tug still afloat but looks hopeless, hope to arrive 0200. Tug will require to be beached, badly down by the head'. The *Bramley* was eventually brought in and beached in St Mary's Pool, where she was patched up and then escorted to Plymouth.

To give some idea of the involvement and intense nature of what RNAPS St Mary's was doing at sea, as distinct from the priorities of RNAS seaplanes on Tresco in the U-boat war, the following patrol reports detail just eleven intense days' activities that August:

HM Trawler *Foss*, part of the RNAPS trawler fleet at St Mary's. *(St Mary's Museum, Isles of Scilly)*

3 August 1917 – All thirty-seven crew from SS *Beechpark* landed in one boat at Porthcressa. Vessel was torpedoed and sunk at 2230, 2 August, 4.5 miles S x E of Peninnis light. Vessel sank in five minutes. Tug *Iago* left for Penzance with crew of the *Beechpark*. HM Armed Yacht *Venetia* arrived in harbour to escort the SS *Kathlamba*.

6 August – Collier SS *Fellside* arrived in harbour to load cargo off the SS *A.B. Sherman*.

8 August – Intercepted message from HMS *Dunraven*, 'Am

engaging enemy submarine 48°N, 7.37′W, abandoning ship', Message received later from HMS *Attack*, 'Request tugs sent at once to tow in torpedoed ship, 48° 5N, 7.37′W. [Author's note: *Dunraven* was the decoy ship *Q-5*, armed with 1 x 4-inch, 4 x 12-pounder guns, plus two torpedo tubes and four depth charges, with a redundant 2.5-inch stern gun mounted for show. She also had a high-pressure steam pipe laid around her engine room hatch at deck level which was perforated at regular intervals, so that if she was attacked a valve on the bridge could be opened and steam would engulf the centre of the ship, making her look disabled. Captain Gordon Campbell VC DSO RN was her commanding officer. He had recently been awarded the Victoria Cross and promoted from commander following his destruction of *U-29* when she attacked his *Q-4* the SS *Pargust* on 7 June. The *Pargust* was at 51°N, 11′W, when attacked and managed to pump over forty shells into the U-boat, most of them into her conning tower, killing her captain in the first few minutes.]

Dunraven was attacked by *U-21* on 8 August, a shell from the submarine detonating one of her depth-charges, blowing away part of her stern along with one of her hidden 4-inch guns and gun crew. The U-boat then submerged and the expected torpedo struck amidships, after which the German vessel surfaced and machine gunned the ship's boats that supposedly held all the crew, being unaware Captain Campbell and several guns crew were still hidden on board. The Q-ship then fired both of her torpedoes at the submarine narrowly missing their target, after which *U-21* shelled the freighter till the USS *Noma* and HM destroyers *Attack* and *Christopher* arrived. The *Christopher* took the wreck of the *Dunraven* in tow, and got her to a point 60 miles west of Ushant when tugs from Plymouth arrived. At 0130 on 8 August the destroyer went alongside and took off the remaining crew just as the *Dunraven* was about to capsize. Now a floating and dangerous derelict, a depth charge was dropped alongside and the *Dunraven*'s hull was shelled until she sank. Captain Campbell received a second bar to his DSO, Lieutenant Bonner and Petty Officer Pitcher both

Six Royal Navy armed motor launches in Padstow harbour on the north coast of Cornwall. These craft and others based at Newlyn and Penzance, carried out anti-submarine patrols as far afield as the Isles of Scilly supporting the RNAPS, St Mary's. *(Penlee House Gallery & Museum, Percy Sharp Collection)*

received the Victoria Cross (VC), whilst other crew members were awarded the DSO or DSC for gallantry.

15 August – Trawler No.3293 *Saurian* returned to port with thirty-one survivors from the SS *Asti*, sunk by torpedo 220 miles SW of Scilly. Wireless message intercepted from HMS *Laertes*, 'SS *Eastgate* torpedoed amidships at 1030, floating well and consider could be towed in.' Intercepted from HMS *Brisk*, the SS *Delphic* torpedoed position 47° 47′N, 08° 33′W; tugs *Danube II* and *Gladstone* sent to assist.

17 August – HMS *Laertes* reported 10 miles SE of St Mary's with SS *Eastgate* in tow, requires assistance to enter harbour. Drifter *Rambling Rose* and salvage vessel *Ranger* proceeding. Instructions issued to all trawlers to use hydrophones on every patrol.

18 August – Intercepted message from HM Destroyer

Armed motor launch ML579 in Holman's dry dock at Penzance for maintenance. All the trawlers and drifters based at St Mary's used this dock for repairs and routine inspections. *(Penlee House Gallery & Museum, Percy Sharp Collection)*

Christopher, 'urgent, SS *Penhurst* torpedoed in No.2 hold, water gaining, standing by at 47° 38′N, 19′W, request tugs. Making for Falmouth 4 knots. *Penhurst* now in tow of *Sun II*, two trawlers in company making for Plymouth.'

19 August – Intercepted message from Falmouth that *Delphic* sank at 2200. Informed Admiral, Devonport that tug *Sun II* had grounded on a rock when beaching the *Eastgate*, and unable to refloat her this tide. Tug *Zaree* has part crew of the *Delphic* on board. Trawlers No.1191 *Whitefriars* and No.1359 *City of Edinburgh* arrived from sea and reported having seen an oiler, name unknown, sunk by enemy submarine at 47° 32′N, 08° 43′W on 17 August at noon. Chased submarine for one and a half hours, fired six rounds at extreme range. Returned to wreckage but unable to ascertain name of ship or any sign of her crew. Vessel set on fire before she sank.

20 August – No.1191 *Whitefriars* and No.1359 *City of Edinburgh* with tug *Sun II* proceeding to assistance of SS *Penhurst*. Message intercepted from HMS *Jurassic*, 'am being shelled by submarine 49°42′N, 05° 48′W.' Trawlers No.3293 *Saurian* and No.1360 *Nancy Hague* proceeded to investigate. Tresco seaplane 8680 reports dropping 2 x 100lb bombs on enemy submarine at 0945 in position 94-PWN. Bombs exploded ahead of wash when submarine had dived, no sign of debris or oil observed after attack.'

24 August – Intercepted message from destroyer USS *Allen*, 'steamer *War Captain*, engines broken down position 49° 55′N, 08° 34′W, at 2300, trawlers need to screen vessel. Send tugs when weather moderates.' HMS *Leonidas* reported via the SS *Valetta* that a large steamship was sunk at 1315, no sign of any boats. Trawler No 1359 *City of Edinburgh* sent to investigate.

26 August – Intercepted from HMS *Acasta*, 'I have been in collision with unknown steamer off Scilly, collision bulkhead buckled. The SS *Bayholel* requires assistance, am standing by her.' HMS *Midge* reported Italian SS *Juno* disabled at 48° 45′N, 07° 20′W, requires immediate assistance, position one mile west of Wolf Rock. Tug *Zaras* sent to assist. Land's End Radio reported 'Captain's boat from the torpedoed *Malda* picked up by destroyer USS *Cassin*, four boats still adrift making for Scilly.'

27 August – Trawler No.3278 *Foss* reports picking up part crew of the French SS *Henrietta*, torpedoed 24 August, 'one boat still adrift, should I proceed Penzance?' Trawler No.1361 *Hercules IV* arrived in port with twenty-eight survivors from the *Malda*. Survivors of *Malda* sent to Penzance on board the SS *Lyonesse*.

And so it went on, day after day, ships torpedoed out in the cold Atlantic, men who slept night after night fully dressed being thrown into the sea, scalded or incinerated in engine rooms, trapped below deck as their ships went down, or cast adrift in small boats open to the elements. The RNAPS organisation on St Mary's and the RNAS on Tresco, worked day and night at full stretch, answering radio signals, sending out trawlers, drifters, rescue tugs and floatplanes to assist, attacking U-boats, deterring others, and maintaining their aircraft and twenty trawlers and drifters which were bringing back countless injured seamen.

Whilst the trench warfare in Belgium and France some 320 miles away to the east was bad enough, even if Scillonian soldiers recuperating from wounds at home or on their precious seven days leave granted every two years were prepared to talk about their experiences, the Atlantic war on Scilly's doorstep brought home to everyone on the islands the reality of the war at sea.

The cap badge worn by senior and junior rates of the Royal Naval Air Service. The eagle symbol was eventually incorporated into the cap badge of the Royal Air Force when the two organisations amalgamated. *(Richard Larn Collection)*

If it is possible to discriminate between the degrees of danger the crews of merchant ships faced, then those in their engine and boiler rooms were at most risk, which included engineers, oilers, boiler men, trimmers, stokers and donkey men. They worked alongside boilers and machinery full of superheated high-pressure steam. When a torpedo slammed into the side of a merchant ship and its 250kg warhead detonated tearing a 15m wide hole, not only did the sea flood in leaving little time for the 'black gang' to escape up near vertical ladders, but the explosion would wreck boilers and pipes. Men at work wearing only trousers and singlets due to the heat were exposed to terrible scalding and burns, the most painful of all injuries. The countless lifeboats that reached St Mary's carrying survivors would have had more than their share of injured men, including engine room staff with terrible burns. None of the surviving records make much mention of the hospital staff on St Mary's and what they endured in those dark days, but Lemon Hall and Holgate's Hotel must have witnessed countless harrowing scenes with the nurses, VADs, helpers and Dr Addison stretched to their limits. Fortunately, the introduction of organized convoys for merchant ships, which were now escorted more than half way across the Atlantic, had an immediate impact on ship losses, reducing the numbers by over 50 per cent immediately. It is true to say that late 1917 was a turning point in the Atlantic war.

Whilst the magistrates had imposed a ban on late pub opening hours earlier in the year, the Defence of the Realm Act, para 10 was then implemented, which limited mid-day drinking hours from noon to 2.30pm. Treating others to drinks was strictly forbidden and evening opening hours were restricted from 6pm to 9.30pm.

Many items of cargo were now being washed ashore all around Scilly, including dozens of dead horses and mules on Bryher and St Agnes that had to be buried. Barrels of lard also washed in, and if the staves were damaged they attracted the attention of seagulls who gorged on the contents. Islanders referred to these as 'lumps' or 'snowballs'. If they could get one home without alerting the Customs officers, they melted the lard down in pans to eliminate sand and stones. Great slabs of expensive candle wax measuring 18in by 8in and 2in thick came ashore for a time, which were melted down and poured into candle moulds, saving the islanders money. If lard or candlewax was declared to the Customs officers they were sold by auction, the salvor receiving one third of the overall sum raised. On the off islands, when the remains of ships' lifeboats were washed up, their emergency lockers under the thwarts frequently held sealed tins of thick, hard, ship's biscuit, 8lb tins of dried vegetables or a dried meat compound known as Pemmican, all of which were welcome additions to an already lean Scillonian diet.

On 26 July the Church Lads' Brigade on St Mary's was inspected by Brigadier General Porter, who reported:

'This Company was thoroughly inspected in Swedish drill, general turn out, steadiness on parade, elementary drill, signaling, shooting, marching and average attendance. I was quite satisfied with all I saw except their shooting, and in that they did not seem to have had sufficient practice. The average

The entire ship's company of RNAS Tresco outside the maintenance hangar.
(St Mary's Museum, Isles of Scilly)

score was under 50%. The Unit has been thoroughly grounded in elementary work, and great credit is due to Captain Jeffery, who has kept the Unit together under difficult circumstances. I strongly recommend that this Company be formed into a Cadet Corp, Company F, which will admit boys of all denominations and probably largely increase their number. All Church Lads Cadet Corps have been affiliated to the King's Own Rifle Corp.'

Regarding events at RNAS Tresco, Flight Sub Lieutenant Anderson's log books and others which survive at the Fleet Air Arm Museum, Yeovilton, cover the period from the arrival of the first H-12 aircraft to Armistice Day 1918. In addition to details of day to day events, including attacks on German U-boats, these logs give us a snapshot of life on Tresco for the Royal Navy personnel stationed there but are obviously too detailed to record in full. The following are a selection of flight reports, illustrating the contribution RNAS Tresco was making to the Atlantic war.

21 August – H-12 aircraft, No.8680, manned by Flight Lieutenant Hoare and Flight Sub Lieutenant Forsyth were on a routine patrol 55 mile SSW of Scilly when they saw a submarine six miles away steering NNE which then submerged. They dropped 3 x 100lb bombs, all of which exploded, but nothing more was seen of the submarine, nor any floating debris.

18 September – Capsized ship and two lifeboats with crews seen close to the coast.

14 October – H-12, No.8680, Flight Lieutenant McGill pilot, Flight Sub Lieutenant Anderson, Lieutenant Atkinson and Air Mechanic Pike, when seven miles off the Scillies, found a submarine on the surface which then submerged. Two red Very [sometimes spelled Verey] lights fired to alert nearby trawlers, then dropped 4 x 100lb bombs which fell clear of the U-boat by several yards. Circled and dropped calcium flares, sending W/T calls to all ships at 1558, warned armed yacht approaching the area of submarine's presence.

18 October – H-12 No.8686, Flight Lieutenant McGill and Flight Sub-Lieutenant Morgan-Smith, saw a submarine 30 miles SW of Bishop Rock. With the submarine's periscope still awash, they passed directly overhead and dropped 4 x 100lb bombs, which exploded close together and just ahead of the periscope, large quantities of oil and bubbles on the surface; category 'possible damage'.

The seaplanes left on moorings in Tresco Channel were frequently subjected to extreme weather. On 16 December several of the large H-12 twin engine biplanes lifted completely off the surface of the sea into the air like huge kites, which then broke their holding lines falling back into the sea before being blown ashore upside down, badly damaged, only their engines worth recovering. In anticipation that the Germans might put a landing party ashore to blow up the RNAS W/T station, Tresco was now guarded at night by shore patrols accompanied by dogs.

The inside of one of the ten junior ratings' buildings at RNAS Tresco, the beds are not left made up when not in use, and the only heating is the cast iron stove which burned coke. *(Penlee House Gallery & Museum, Percy Sharp Collection)*

Although not one case of a conscientious objection has been found in the Magistrates Court records on Scilly, the Military Court representative did bring a case to Scilly on 26 September objecting to the exemption of six months given to R.C. Thomas, aged 25, and Hedley Jenkins, 27, both of St Mary's, on the grounds of their labour being essential to the family flower farms. It was held that bulb growing 'was only a luxury in time of war'. The court held that the young men should join up in the ordinary way and they were soon on board the *Lyonesse* bound for Penzance.

On 20 September the Council of the Isles of Scilly held a long debate on the shortage of domestic coal on the islands and the difficulties in obtaining supplies. Without mains electricity, coal was essential for cooking, washing and heating. The chairman said it might be possible to obtain coal through the Admiralty. Mr Clement Thomas, having purchased a small vessel, said he was prepared to fill her with coal at Penzance and bring it over on a regular basis, an offer which the council agreed to accept, but with the current shortage had already asked the Admiralty to use one of their colliers to land 200 tons on the quay at St Mary's, from where the council would arrange distribution as long as there was an increase in the price to cover the working expenses.

Although the council and the general public had been made aware that the ferry SS *Lyonesse* was to be sold, it came as a shock when Mr Banfield, the owner, sold her to a company in Queenstown, Eire, in October for £18,000, nearly twice as much as he had paid for her when new in 1887, thirty years earlier. Thereafter the Ministry of Shipping made drifters and trawlers as well as the armed collier SS *Artificer*, available to supply the islands and transport passengers, the government giving notice that the service would be withdrawn at the end of the war. In fact it withdrew the service when RNAS/RAF Tresco closed. At the same time Commander Oliver RN, had put out a notice saying that civilians were not to use the vessels plying between Scilly and Penzance without his written permission.

On September 7, the Portuguese sailing schooner *Rio Mondego* was towed in from the Atlantic derelict and run ashore off Samson, whilst on passage from Lisbon to New York with a cargo of port wine. She had been captured by a German U-boat some 25 miles SW of Scilly, the enemy making the Portuguese crew abandon ship before placing explosive charges down in her hold at the base of her masts, but being built of wood she refused to sink. An elderly local, Tom Pender, was installed on board by the Customs officer in a cabin on the upper deck as a caretaker. His task was to stop pilfering. One evening a naval officer from Tresco organized a small boat party and, accompanied by six officers and four sergeants, they boarded the wreck, bringing with them an assortment of containers. As they approached the ship the caretaker shouted, 'No one is

The wreck of the wine laden Portuguese schooner *Rio Mondego* at anchor off the island of Samson. This became a 'private wine cellar' for RNAS Tresco. *(Mike Harcum Collection)*

The upper deck of the *Rio Mondego* wreck.

"The Work of the Huns."

allowed on board here', to which he received the reply, 'We are short of water', the boat promptly pulling alongside. One of the officers disappeared into the caretaker's cabin with Pender, waving a wad of papers, and shortly after emerged and told the remainder to come aboard. Using brute force and ignorance, they managed to get a barrel floating in the hold out and onto the deck, where it was broached and filled their numerous bottles, flasks, buckets, cans and dixies. The raiding party left at 9pm, the caretaker now the worse for drink, as were several of the servicemen. The wreck was subsequently raided several times for her wine. It was said that on Armistice Day, 90 per cent of the Tresco servicemen were intoxicated due of the quantity of wine they had taken from the wreck and hidden.

RNAPS had a very busy 24 hours on 1 October commencing with No.1191 *Whitefriars* reporting by W/T from sea she had a capsized derelict vessel carrying oil in 48.21N, 08.56W, and had fired three explosive charges against the hull to sink her but with no success and requested instructions. The Admiral, Devonport, ordered two tugs to sea to the derelict with a view to demolishing or towing her to the nearest port. *Whitefriars* then reported she had picked up five crew of the French fishing vessel *Sainte Pierre*, sunk by submarine in area 39-JSD and that there were still five boats adrift somewhere holding twenty-one men. HMS *Forester* then radioed St Mary's that she had another derelict sailing vessel at 48.30N, 08.12W to which the crew refused to return. 'Have taken *Whitefriars* and *Nancy Hague* under my orders to tow her in.' *Whitefriars* then reported that a submarine was approaching an American schooner about 15 miles SE of St Mary's and that seaplanes on Scilly should be informed. The Devonport tug *Revenger* succeeded in towing the derelict into Crow Sound, despite the fact it had capsized the moment the tow commenced. HM Tug *Bramley Moore* then arrived at St Mary's with eight crew of the American schooner *Annie F. Conlon*.

All other trawlers were reported to be in port, refuelling or resting, No.1360 *Nancy Hague*, having been at sea eight days and

If the RNAPS or RNAS were reasonably sure they had sunk a German U-boat, a Royal Navy 'standard' diver, wearing a copper helmet, would be put down on the wreck to identify it and, if possible, enter the submarine and secure documentation, log books and charts. *(Penlee House Gallery & Museum, Percy Sharp Collection)*

nights, and No.1191*Whitefriars* six days. Tugs *Bramley Rose* and *Epic* left St Mary's to meet Mercantile Convoy HN-11 out off the Bishop Rock. [Author's note: by 7 October the *Annie F. Conlon* was anchored inside the Hats Buoy, Crow Sound, but lying on her beam ends.]

On 6 December, St Mary's intercepted a radio message from

Newlyn Harbour in early 1918, showing the vast number of armed trawlers, drifters and motor launches either based there or at Penzance, as part of the anti-submarine organisation. *(Penlee House Gallery & Museum, Percy Sharp Collection)*

HMS *Spitfire*, addressed to the Admiral, Devonport stating 'tugs recalled, returned to port 1010.'

A coast watcher on St Martin's then reported heavy gunfire about 15 miles north of the island. Seaplane No.8680 returning from patrol was sent to investigate, but got back at 1315 with nothing to report. In fact she had narrowly missed the destruction of the USS *Jacob Jones*, a four-funnel Conyngham Class American escort destroyer based at Queenstown, Eire. In company with six other destroyers she was returning to base following convoy escort duty off Brest, when *U-53* fired a torpedo which struck her stern at 1625. The racks on her stern holding depth charges, primed and ready for use, exploded underwater as she sank, killing most of her 108 crew who were now in the water. She took just eight minutes to sink, 25 miles SE of the Bishop Rock.

Church Magazine No.155 of November was bemoaning that with carbide no longer available, *'we have had to rehang the old oil lamps in the churches and we were wise to have kept them.'*

There were many houses on St Mary's that Christmas whose curtains remained drawn as news of loved ones killed or missing slowly filtered through. Private Wilfred Ellis had been killed in action whilst doing sentry duty in late June, aged 23; Private Walter Franklin had been killed in action and Walter Nicholls was reported missing. Seaman Edward Ashford died at sea; Private Roger Nicholls and Private Cyril Martin Lakey, aged 22, Duke of Cornwall's Light Infantry from Tresco were killed in action and William Mitchell wounded. Private Frederick Ashford died in hospital of wounds that May, along with Private Frederick Nicholls, whilst Private Albert Stanley Deason lost a foot whilst in the trenches. William Routling, Royal Navy, was wounded in November; Private Frank Pender, aged 27, was killed in action that December, whilst Privates Reginald Woodcock and Albert Nance were badly gassed and wounded respectively.

Postcard home from Private Frank Pender, 210th Battalion Canadian Army. Born at Maypole, St Mary's, emigrated to Canada with his brother William. Enlisted at Moose Jaw, Saskatchewan, 1916. Transferred to the 46th Battalion, Canadian Infantry. Died of wounds 1917, buried in Nine Elms Cemetery, Poperinghe, Belgium. *(John & Kay Banfield)*

CHAPTER 5

1918
The tide turns

Residents on the Isles of Scilly were stunned to hear of the untimely death of Percy Thomas Chirgwin JP, aged 52. Percy Chirgwin was a successful business man living in Penzance who ran four general grocery stores in West Cornwall and one at the Bank, Hugh Town, St Mary's which survives to this day as a clothing/gift shop called The Sandpiper. Heritage demands today mean that an original name board advertising 'R. Chirgwin & Son, Provision Merchants and Agents for W.&A. Gilbey' still sits proudly over the façade of this old shop.

On Sunday, 31 January, Mr Chirgwin, having paid a visit to his store in Scilly, joined other passengers on board the armed replacement ferry *Artificer*, to return home to Penzance. He elected to remain outside on deck, but when the ship was some two miles off Peninnis Head a heavy sea struck her side causing him to fall overboard. The vessel was immediately stopped, went astern to get closer to him and a lifebelt was thrown which he got hold of. He then lay floating on his back awaiting rescue. The ship's lifeboat was launched and Mr Chirgwin was recovered alive, but by now unconscious. Taken below to a cabin and wrapped in blankets, all efforts to restore him failed. It was assumed he had died from the shock of immersion in a wintery sea. The *Artificer* returned to St

This Hugh Town shop, which now sells clothing, still carries its original Chirgwin & Son sign board, the owner at the time losing his life when he fell overboard from the islands' ferry. *(Richard Larn Collection)*

Mary's quay where the body was landed and taken to Tregarthen's Hotel, of which he had been a director. An entry in the Church Magazine of February 1918 reads: *'The death of Mr P. Chirgwin came as a shock to us all. He was so well known in the islands that he was almost looked on as a Scillonian.'*

Government surplus goods, which were something quite new and a novelty at the time, were now being offered through advertisements in Penzance newspapers. On 21 February readers were offered, *'Army boots for sale – will stand any amount of hard wear, just the thing for Tram and Bus men, farm workers etc. 9 shillings 6d a pair, carriage paid.'* Sales were obviously not that good since exactly a month later the advertisement had changed to read, *'Repaired Army Boots for sale, absolutely good as new, new soles and heels, uppers guaranteed. 8 shillings 11p, carriage 7d extra.'* Troops at the front and relatives were also beginning to consider personal safety, as advertisements commenced to appear for personal protective clothing:

> **'Dayfield Body Shield** – *the best shield for the men at the front. No bayonet thrust can penetrate it, also proof against shrapnel, hand grenades, shell and bomb splinters, can stop a revolver bullet at close range. Weighs only 5¾lbs, and can be worn under the tunic, protecting back and front 17ins x 12ins. Have you protected him as much as you can? Made in London, 52 shillings 6d each.'*

On the general war front it was reported that Canadian shipyards were making good some of our losses, having just finished the first of an order for eight new vessels. The order, placed by the Imperial Munitions Board was for an overall total of eighty-seven ships, many built in the United States, which were classified as British Standard Ships, dry cargo vessels of 8,800 tons, all built exactly the same and given the prefix 'War' to their names, i.e: *War Harbour, War Haven, War Wave* etc.

In France, on 21 March it was reported that Paris had been shelled at 15-minute intervals for several hours by a long range German gun 75 miles (120km) distant, which was 12 miles behind the enemy lines. The shells were 9.20ins diameter (23.5cm), filled with a bursting charge of 40lbs, fired at an elevation of 60°, which meant that at one point the shells reached a height of 38.5 miles (62km)! This was the weapon the Kaiser had commissioned known as 'Big Bertha', which was eventually intended to be used to shell London from across the Channel. In the House of Commons Lloyd George raised the age for military service to 50, and in special cases even 55 years, which denuded Scilly of even more men.

Whilst the patrol trawlers based at Scilly no longer escorted as many individual ships as the trawlers based at Penzance and Falmouth did, the RNAPS Scillies weekly report for 5 January 1918

RNAS Tresco in its early days, with only five small wooden sheds in which to store aircraft, a small wooden slipway, and an old gig shed centre right. Far left are the remains of a crashed aircraft, and far right the *Sophie* shipwreck. *(Fleet Air Arm Museum)*

shows that on 19 December 1917, No.1191 *Whitefriars* and No.1359 *Cambria* had been dispatched to escort the SS *South Pacific*, which was somewhere down in the Bay of Biscay on her way from Dakar to Falmouth. Three days later, having failed to find her and with the trawlers low on coal, No.3293 *Saurian* and No.1360 *Nancy Hague* were sent to relieve them, with *Whitefriars* and *Cambria* still looking for the ship on 2 January. The following day, the relief trawlers having arrived on site at 49° 50′N, the other two set off for Scilly meeting up with the *South Pacific* two miles

SW of the Bishop Rock and escorted her to Plymouth, arriving on 4 January. *Saurian* and *Nancy Hague* were then informed and told to continue with a normal patrol.

The destroyer HMS *Furious* struck the Crim in January and had to be towed through Broad Sound to St Mary's, where she was berthed alongside the quay awaiting inspection by divers and repairs. The report ends with a summary of the days the trawlers had spent at sea: *Whitefriars* – 7: *Cambria* – 7; *Foss* – 4: *City of Edinburgh* – 4; *Saurian* – 5: *Nancy Hague* – 5; *Hercules IV* – (relieving at Penzance). Meanwhile the armed motor launches based at Newlyn were going to sea daily carrying out hydrophone sweeps in the Channel, looking for submarines or minesweeping.

A group of nineteen Royal Navy officers who were some of the crew on board armed HM Motor Launches based in Newlyn Harbour. Up to twenty-five MLs were based here at one time from late 1916. The building on the quay to the right was wardroom accommodation for these officers. (*Penlee Gallery, Sharp Collection*)

A Short 357, Type 184 floatplane in the process of being recovered after landing on the sea. *(Fleet Air Arm Museum)*

It is interesting to compare what the trawlers based at Scilly were achieving compared to those at Falmouth, Penzance, Newlyn and Padstow. The summary of enemy submarines sighted for the week ending 12 January 1918 included in the Falmouth RNAPS weekly reports:

6 January – Land's End radio intercepted a message from the USS *Benham*, 'At 0145, 50° 30′N, 07° 08′W, unsuccessful attack made by submarine on convoy. USS *Parker* dropped three depth charges. No sign of submarine afterwards.'

Number of vessels escorted during the week: From Mount's Bay – 45; from Brest – 62; other vessels – 4; losses – nil, [which shows the convoy system was already having a positive effect]. Information was received at 1645 on 7 January from St Ives War Signal Station, regarding Swedish SS *Carolus* in distress off Godrevy. Trawlers No.3508 *John Kidd* and No.1758 *Slebech* with tug *Epic* were sent to her assistance, but in high seas, the crew having abandoned ship since she had a heavy list, nothing could be done. The *Carolus* drove ashore on a sandy beach under Hayle Battery practically undamaged and was later refloated.

At 0200 on 8 January, information received that the SS *Taihayi* was leaking badly with fires out at 49° 16′N, 09° 28′W and required assistance. Tugs *Blazer* and *Revenger* were sent from Scilly and succeeded in getting vessel in tow. They attempted to reach Queenstown, but she sank at 1430 on 9 January. At 1000 on 9 January Norwegian SS *Ula* was torpedoed and sank 10 miles ESE of the Lizard. The crew was brought into Falmouth by patrol vessels. 11 January, convoy OF-20 sailed. Enemy submarine activity had decreased considerably. By now, the Falmouth RNAPS complement of trawlers was forty-eight, compared to Scilly's twenty vessels.

After the United States entered the war, US Navy Armed Motor Launches were also based at Newlyn. These were larger than Royal Navy launches but were not good sea-boats, having been designed for inland waterways and estuary patrols, not the open sea of the Western Approaches. *(Penlee House Gallery & Museum, Percy Sharp Collection)*

The services' shop on Tresco, selling tobacco, confectionary, biscuits, snacks and soft drinks,which was the equivalent of a WW2 Navy, Army & Airforce Institution (NAAFI) shop, which first opened in 1921. *(St Mary's Museum, Isles of Scilly)*

Whilst there is no mention of any increase in armament being fitted to the trawlers and drifters stationed at St Mary's until much later in the year, which was probably due to availability, there is every reason to believe that they now had increased capabilities to attack submarines. From October 1916 all crews of the RNR Trawler Division were given 28-day training courses in gunnery at HMS *Excellent*, Portsmouth, or else Chatham and Devonport. This qualified them as Special Gunners (Trawler) (SGT) which for the first time qualified them for gunnery payment. The courses included instruction in 4-inch guns and below, but particularly howitzers and bomb-throwers, newly developed anti-submarine weapons. A large proportion of the course was devoted to actual firing practice, and selected men were given an additional nine days of shooting instruction, which was spent at gun drill, stripping and ammunition handling. The new weapons being fitted to trawlers in particular included conventional depth-charges, whilst Lewis guns were only issued to auxiliary patrol vessels. Motor Launches and Q-Ships from 1917 onwards had either 7.5inch or 11-inch howitzers or 9.5-inch bomb-throwers manufactured by Messrs. Thorneycroft. From these evolved the highly successful Vickers 10-inch bomb-thrower, 750 of which were fitted in 1917 and were probably here on Scilly.

The War Office recognised the importance of RNAS Tresco as a base vital in the fight against U-boats now that the United States had entered the war, causing more and more troopships and supply vessels to cross the Atlantic. On 31 March Flight Commander J. Cripps based at Tresco was promoted to command the RAF base at Plymouth, his place being taken by Flight Commander R. Maycock, who had ambitions to increase the size of RAF Tresco. His proposals were endorsed by Captain Gerrard of the SW Group Headquarters, himself originally a RNAS pilot in 1911 and one of Chief of the Air Staff, Sir Hugh Trenchard's early instructors at the world's first military flying school at Upavon. Unfortunately for Maycock, a request to build a second slipway and erect another large steel-framed hangar, which would have meant demolishing the Palace Row block of cottages on Tresco, was not sanctioned by Tresco Estate.

The weekly reports of RNAPS Scilly had this to say:

5 January 1918 – *Foss* and No.1359 *City of Edinburgh* proceeded to sea on patrol.

No.1191 *Whitefriars* and No.1358 *Cambria* in port. Tugs *Epic* and *Revenger* called to assistance of SS *Rewa* (hospital ship), torpedoed off Hartland Point at 0815, but were recalled at 1440 on hearing the *Rewa* had sunk. No.1360 *Nancy Hague* and No.3293 *Saurian* arrived in port.

6 January – *Whitefriars* and *Cambria* patrolling Section E, *Foss* patrolling Y.

7 January – No.1361 *Hercules IV* patrolling Section Y. *Saurian* and *Nancy Hague* proceeding to intercept and escort SS *Crown of Seville* or SS *Helmsdale*. Tug *Epic* sailed for St Ives in accordance with Admiralty Message 1365 of 5 January, and later sailed from St Ives to the assistance of *Carolus*, five miles NNW of Godrevy Light.

The motor transport pool of RNAS Tresco, showing range of six early cars and lorries. *(St Mary's Museum, Isles of Scilly)*

An early steam driven solid tyre Foden lorry, part of the RNAS Tresco motor pool fleet, which appears to have become bogged down in mud. *(St Mary's Museum, Isles of Scilly)*

8 January – Tugs *Blazer* and *Revenger* sailed to assistance of SS *Taihayi*. Leaking seriously and fires out in position 49° 16′N, 09° 28′W. *Foss* and *Hercules* patrolling Section Y. *Saurian* and *Nancy Hague* escort duties. *Whitefriars* and *Cambria* in port. *City of Edinburgh* refitting.

9 January – Tugs *Blazer* and *Revenger* towing *Taiyihi* to Queenstown. *Whitefriars* and *Cambria* endeavoring to intercept and escort SS *Viana* and vessels listed in DRL.46.

Foss and *Hercules IV* in port. *Saurian* and *Nancy Hague* endeavoring to pick up SS *Helmsdale*.

10 January – Tugs *Blazer* and *Revenger* returned to port, the SS *Taiyihi* having sunk, after picking up twenty bags of mails which were sent to Penzance after being handed over to the Post Office authorities. *Whitefriars, Cambria, Sauriuan* and *Nancy Hague* on escort duties. *Saurian* returned to base being unable to pick up the SS *Helmsdale*. [Author's note: with no mention of other trawlers in the weekly report it would appear the total number was temporarily reduced to seven.]

11 January – the Scilly trawler *Whitefriars* was sent out to pick up the Norwegian sailing ship *Manicia*, which was in tow of the tug *Racia. Whitefriars* met up with them three miles SW the Seven Stones light vessel and escorted both to Sharpness.

A Curtiss H-12, large America seaplane with a maintenance crew, who have just fitted a new port side propeller. *(Fleet Air Arm Museum)*

1 March – Trawler 1191 *Whitefriars* returned from Buncrana (northern Ireland) at noon, after taking a cargo of towing hawsers to that base. At 1415 on 19 February, position 52° 02′N, 05° 48′W, *Whitefriars* sighted a submarine bearing N30° 00′W, firing on a small steamer. The trawler opened fire with her 6-pounder gun at 6,000 yards, shells falling some 3,000 yards short. After firing seventeen rounds the submarine increased the distance between them, and *Whitefriars* ceased firing. The submarine then closed in on the steamer at high speed and fired into her at short range, hitting her waterline and setting fire to the bridge. *Whitefriars* picked up eight survivors, the ship being the *Wheat Flower*, from Newport with coal; at 1515 the vessel sank.

No.3278 *Foss* and No.1359 *City of Edinburgh II* intended carrying out firing practice at 1000 Monday, 25 February in position 10 miles south of the Bishop Rock, but were unable to do so on account of bad weather.

5 March – Trawler *Whitefriars* sighted enemy submarine at 49° 48′N, 06°W and at full speed opened fire at extreme range, firing ten rounds, all of which fell short. At 1105 submarine submerged steering north. At 1125 when over the position the submarine last seen, *Whitefriars* dropped D depth charge set to 80ft. Altered course to southward and dropped G depth charge. Altered course to west and dropped a further D depth charge, then stopped and kept hydrophone watch until noon. Remained in vicinity until 1930 but nothing further was heard or seen of the submarine.

Trawlers No.3278 *Foss* and No.1359 *City of Edinburgh* carried out exploratory mine sweeping. Trawlers swept in and out of St Mary's Channel, five miles to seaward and back. Sweeping discontinued due to a gale.

A 12-pounder, 12cwt gun has arrived at the Base for trawler *Whitefriars*. Rescue tug *Bramley Moore* fitted with two Type G depth charges on 6 March.

20 March – A Petty Officer RNR gunnery rating has been allowed to the Base, and has carried out most useful instruction during the week.

Trawler No.1360 *Nancy Hague* fitted with W/T (Wireless Telegraphy); No.3278 *Foss* and No.1360 *Nancy Hague*, No.3293 *Saurian* and No.1191 *Whitefriars*, now all fitted with Single Towed Charge. Drifter No.2565 *Marvellous* is fitted with one 6-pounder HA gun (high angle) and not with 3-pounder.

5 April – At 1000 BST on Monday, 1 April, trawlers No.3278 *Foss* and No.1359 *City of Edinburgh* carried out firing practice 10 miles south of Bishop Rock; 20 rounds 1-inch Aiming Rifle and 4 rounds 12-pounder. Two hits recorded. Trawler *City of Edinburgh* fired 16 rounds Aiming Tube and four of Practice Shot, scoring five hits. Range: 600 to 1400 yards. Good shooting, very difficult due to heavy swell. All gun crews in port given instruction in the Spotting Table and Gun Drill.

10 May – Section Y has been patrolled by two trawlers throughout the week. Operations against enemy vessels – nil; operations against enemy mines – nil. Trawler No.1191 *Whitefriars* has been fitted with 12-pounder, 12cwt gun, P.I. mounting. Trawler No.1358 *Cambria* at Falmouth now being fitted with 12-pounder.

As the war progressed, the armament of RNAPS ships improved as hydrophone detection equipment, net mines, depth charges and finally anti-submarine mortars were introduced. This photograph shows a 9-inch mortar, capable of throwing a mortar bomb some distance from a ship. *(Richard Larn Collection)*

31 May – Operations against enemy vessels – nil; operations against enemy mines – nil. Usual gunnery instructions carried out during the past week and magazines inspected, rockets etc overhauled. Trawler No.1361 *Hercules IV* proceeds to Falmouth on 1 June to be fitted with 12-pounder, 12cwt gun.

21 June – Two trawlers patrolled the North Cornish coast continuously throughout the week. Operations against enemy vessels – nil; operations against enemy mines – nil. Trawler No.1361 *Hercules IV*, 6-pounder QF gun removed and 12-pounder. 12cwt QF gun mounted in lieu during refit of vessel.

It is obvious from June onwards that the intensity of the U-boat war is almost over, since on 3 November Falmouth RNAPS is reporting 'Patrols reduced by 50 per cent as per instructions'. The Scillies' RNAPS reported on 3 November that 'submarine activity entirely suspended'. By 29 November the station's report states, 'Patrols – nil; enemy submarine activity – nil; activity against enemy mines – nil.'

RNAS Tresco continued to grow in size, personnel, aircraft and responsibilities, and on 14 March its first assignment of WRNS arrived. From 1 April 1918 the Royal Naval Air Service ceased to exist, which was the day the Royal Air Force was born, and in August Tresco became 234 Squadron RAF with four flights (Nos. 350-353) under the control of 71 Wing, 9 Group. The establishment of the new squadron called for a change in personnel, so that now there were 33 officers, 21 warrant officers and sergeants, 46 corporals, 202 other ranks, 25 WRAF and 21 women (household cleaners). By way of road transport they had one heavy lorry tender, one motorcycle and sidecar and two Ford cars. F3 flying boats numbered twelve, with several motor launches and one docking lighter. What is not clear is how this change affected the aircrew and maintenance personnel who were technically in the Royal Navy; were the RNAS personnel offered the choice of transfer to the RAF or to remain serving with the Royal Navy? Did that mean an immediate change of uniform and learning a different way to salute? The only comment in the

A group of Royal Navy and Royal Air Force personnel at RNAS Tresco, taken at about the time RNAS was disbanded in favour of the RAF in 1918. *(St Mary's Museum, Isles of Scilly)*

weekly reports was a stoic 'no enthusiasm to become part of the RAF'.

Council minutes tell us that in March an application had been received from the Naval Cricket Club to erect a notice board on the end of a house occupied by Mr McDonald facing Hugh Street. Also that from 15 March the ferry between the islands and Penzance would be run by the Hain Steamship Company of St Ives, to whom all subsidies should be paid in future. No reply had been received from that company regarding the running of the SS *Artificer* or her departure schedule to leave port at some reasonable fixed hour, which was causing bad feelings. The council requested they be granted powers to employ a nurse, which was granted.

A Ministry of Food had been created by the government in 1916 which introduced a voluntary food-rationing scheme, but this failed to work. Forty million Ration Cards valid for sixteen weeks each were then issued in April, which did not come into force until 13 July. Sugar was the first commodity in short supply, which soon extended to butter, marmalade, jam, tea, bacon and meat, the initial

The remains of a Curtiss H-12 seaplane wrecked on the beach, having broken from its mooring in Tresco Channel during a severe gale. *(St Mary's Museum, Isles of Scilly)*

weekly ration per person being 2.5lbs meat and ¾lb of sugar, later reduced to 15ozs of meat, 5ozs of bacon and 4ozs of butter and margarine. New ration books with coupons replaced the ration cards in July, leaving only tea, cheese, coffee and bread unrationed.

A most tragic accident happened around 14 April, which had a devastating effect on both branches of the services on Scilly. Following a concert in the Town Hall, a number of soldiers and sailors on St Mary's were invited to a dance on Tresco, organized by the RNAS. Transport across was provided by one of the patrol drifters. At the end of the dance a large number of servicemen gathered in the canteen, in what is now the New Inn, where beer was available. Eventually, one of the drifter's crew stood up and announced, 'the boat is leaving in half an hour, if you miss it you will be left on Tresco overnight.' Amongst them was a Scotsman Jock Howe and a pianist named Hudson, who commenced to play and soon had a singsong going. The drifter's crewman, who had returned to his boat, was sent back to the canteen by the skipper. He stood in the doorway of the building and shouted, 'the boat is leaving in five minutes.'

Next day four sailors and two soldiers were reported missing to Commander Oliver in the White House, also the fact that a Tresco rowing punt had been taken. The implications were obvious. Several patrol trawlers were sent to sea to search for them, Commander Hope-Vere, Commanding Officer on Tresco offered to put a seaplane up to assist, but the navy were confident they would find them and declined the offer. Unfortunately they found nothing and the men were given up for dead. News was eventually received weeks later, just as the DCLI Regiment to which the two soldiers had belonged was about to leave Scilly, that the boat had been found 200 miles out in the Atlantic, holding just the bodies of two sailors and the cap badges of the two soldiers, Hudson and Howe. What happened will never be known but the tide must have carried the punt up Tresco Channel and out to sea. Without food and water four sailors and two soldiers seemingly died, the last two survivors

Tresco Abbey, the ancestral home of its Duchy tenants, the Dorrien-Smith family. Towards the end of WWI, RNAS Tresco wanted to requisition the building for accommodation, but that was refused. *(Richard Larn Collection)*

having probably heaved the bodies overboard, before finally collapsing into the bottom boards. A memorial service was held for them in the St Mary's church. The regulations regarding parties of servicemen and women travelling between the islands for leisure were immediately tightened up.

Having read through every edition of the *Royal Cornwall Gazette* and the *Cornishman* newspapers for the whole of the war, it was surprising that almost nothing was published in the papers regarding the extensive Patrol Base at Falmouth, nor the smaller one at St Mary's probably due to security regulations. However, one item that found its way into print did so through the Falmouth Magistrates Court since on 18 April one Alfred Capper, an engineer in the patrol service was convicted and fined £10 for aiding and abetting the keeping of a brothel in Falmouth. Lily Hicks, a married woman, was also fined £10 for keeping a brothel at Clovence Terrace, Falmouth.

One of RAF Tresco's flying boats suffered engine trouble and crash landed in the sea near the Bishop on 14 June. Flight Lieutenants Fairhurst and Jenkins and Air Mechanic Wicks were saved, but unfortunately the Wireless Operator, 19-year-old Air Mechanic 3rd Class Arthur Pike, drowned. His name can be found on the Hollybrook War Memorial, Southampton.

Various log books of individual pilots at this time were recording the huge concentration of shipping crossing the Atlantic, entries such as 'twenty-six ships sailing west', and 'twenty-nine assorted ships under escort' and similar, which suggests the convoy system was working. In fact during the last seven months of the war, RAF Tresco recorded only five targets intercepted, of which three were bombed by F.3s, but one, located by an H.12 and another by a Short 225 seaplane dived before they could be bombed. The last accident to a Tresco-based aircraft occurred on 16 July, when Flight Lieutenant Capes, Wireless Operator Hendry and their Short aircraft disappeared, having reported they had lost their bearings and had presumably crashed into the sea. At the time twenty-two aircraft were now based at the air station.

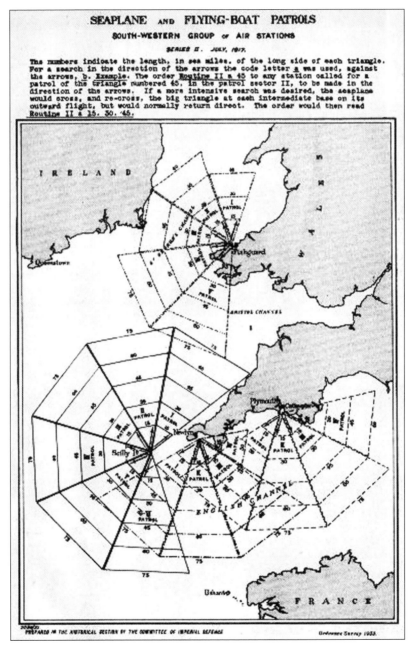

A chart of the air patrol areas covered by RNAS and airships from Plymouth, Newlyn, Isles of Scilly and Fishguard Royal Naval Air Stations. *(Penlee House Gallery & Museum, Percy Sharp Collection)*

Lieutenant Thomas Algernon Smith-Dorrien-Smith of Tresco, had been in failing health for most of the war. His daughters Charlotte and Gwendoline were at Devonport hospital in August when they received news that he was a lot worse. Both girls made their way to Penzance where an armed yacht organized by the Royal Naval Office (RNO), Newlyn, took them to Scilly as soon as possible, but on arrival the Union Jack on Tresco Abbey was already at half-mast, T.A., as he was known, having died on 6 August aged 72, just two days after his son Major Arthur Dorrien-Smith had arrived home on leave.

Later in the autumn, the Smith-Dorrien sisters returned to Tresco with the children from Berkhamstead, the family home, having heard rumours that the air station wanted to take over Tresco Abbey since they were desperately short of accommodation and also that they wanted to demolish Palace Row Cottages in order to erect a second large aircraft hangar. On arrival, intending to use the tower as the nursery, they found that having been shut up for four years the toilet did not work and next day water was running along the passage and down the north stairs. Finally, having settled the nanny and children in the Abbey, the two women returned to London, only to receive a telegram saying that all the Abbey staff and half of the air station were in bed with influenza. One of the sisters promptly returned to Scilly to nurse family 'flu victims only to catch it herself, spending two weeks laid up.

The Abbey must have been in quite a state, since Gwendolyn Smith-Dorrien commented:

'It was the end of the war, and nothing could be got to get the house going. Carpets were all completely worn out and in holes, my sister-in-law having put down a few mats where she could to cover the holes, the Brussels carpets upstairs having come from the cargo of a wrecked ship in Augustus' time, probably some fifty years ago. I bought a carpet at a large price, for the school room. Otherwise I got a blue felt with which I did seven bedrooms and put the odd mats out that

HMS *Pincher*, a Basilisk class destroyer built in 1910, which was wrecked in fog on the Seven Stones Reef, Isles of Scilly, on 24 July 1918. *(Richard Larn Collection)*

were on top. You couldn't get anything. The demobilization was an awful thing, you had to take back anyone who had been with you before the war, and all the riff-raff got left behind. There was fearful discontent in the Air Station and trouble all over the country, because they were furious at some being demobilized and not others, and they set the island on fire twice. They closed another air station on the mainland so we got all their riff-raff sent over here too – the only officers left were terrified of the men.'

The Church Magazine expressed its condolences for the Tresco family and offered a vote of sympathy to Mr Trenear on the loss of his son who was serving in the army, also Mr McFarland for the loss of his son Malcolm, who was Paymaster RNR on board HMS *Cowslip*, an Anchusa class sloop lost at sea on 18 April off Cape

Royal Navy vessels in Newlyn harbour on Armistice Day, celebrating by flying a white ensign over a captured German navy flag. *(Penlee House Gallery & Museum, Percy Sharp Collection)*

Spartel, torpedoed by *UB-105*. Other Scillonians killed that year included Ernest McDonald; Privates Laking and Bristow; Sidney Pender; Hubert Vingo; Thomas Nance; Jack Macklin; Henry Tiffin Trenwith and Wilfred Mortimer.

Tragedy struck the seaplane base on 6 July when the Short 184 seaplane No.2963, which had taken off at 5.30am but returned due to low cloud, took off again at 10.30am. By 3pm the seaplane was in trouble, sending a wireless message that she was going to land on the sea due to an emergency. Nothing further was heard of Second Lieutenant J. Hendry or Observer Lieutenant C. Capes, despite intensive searches by aircraft N2955 and the Felixstowe F.3 No.N4234. The latter also got into difficulties and had to land on the sea close to the hospital ship SS *Braemar Castle* which gave the aircraft a weather lee whilst the two-man crew attempted to effect engine repairs. Heavy seas made it impossible to work and the liner had to take the two men aboard, the aircraft being abandoned.

August 9 was an important day for Tresco. In recognition of the coverage required for their wide-ranging anti-submarine patrols a new unit was formed, 234 Squadron. This dedicated anti-submarine unit with Short 225 seaplanes, did sterling work through to 11 October 1918, when it made the very last attack on a German submarine using a Curtiss H12B, No.4341. The seaplane sighted a U-boat wake four miles ahead of convoy No.HH.71 and managed to drop its bombs on a small oil patch left by the submarine as it dived, but nothing more was seen and the convoy continued unscathed.

The supply of food and coal to Scilly for civilian use was now critical. On 4 August the Council of the Isles of Scilly moved that notices be posted on all the islands requesting that no food stuffs (except perishable things) be exported. It was also resolved that the islands' Food Committee endeavour to find out as nearly as possible, what flour and corn there really were in the islands. Two days later the council was advised that flour in Penzance was £2.8s a sack, that there was a plentiful supply here on the islands for a few weeks but it might be difficult to get any quantity. It had also been found that only recently seven tons of flour had been landed on the islands and enough potatoes to last at least three months. On 25 August the council elected to establish a public office for use of the local fuel overseer in the council buildings, rental to be £6 per annum since at the time there was only one coal

Scillies Patrol & Naval Base Christmas dinner souvenir 1918, listing the names of all vessels whose crews took part, twenty-three ships in total. (*St Mary's Museum, Isles of Scilly*)

Whilst the Council of the Isles of Scilly only received German small arms and trench mortars as war souvenirs to put on public display, many communities received large items such as this 25cms howitzer, known as a *Schwere Minenwerfer* gun, known to British troops as a 'Moaning Minnie'. *(Richard Larn Collection)*

merchant on the islands. Commander Randall RN, commanding officer of the RNAPS, distributed a public notice prohibiting the importation of dogs to the islands, at the same time asking the council for permission to hold dances that coming winter in the Town Hall, which was passed.

Two more feared telegrams were delivered that October: one concerning the death of Hubert Vingoe, the other Roland Gibson.

Hubert was a 2nd steward in the Mercantile Marine, aged 37, Scillonian born. His parents were living at 9 Alma Place, Heamoor, Penzance when they were informed that their son had been killed three years earlier while serving on board the SS *Marquette*. His name appears on the Tower Hill Memorial, London.

The Customs & Excise Schedule Book No.10, concerning Wreck, Salvage and Fees commencing 30 July, held in the St Mary's Museum Library, reveals some of the items washing up on Scillies beaches from sunken ships, although much would not have been declared but hidden away. On 30 July Osbert Hicks handed in a cask of oil for which he received £1.4s.4d; the same day Alfred Pender reported a bale of rubber he had found, receiving £2.11s.9d; John Ellis, Osbert Hicks and G. Franklin, all reported casks of oil, and were paid £1.4s.4d, whilst John Ellis, who had found five casks, was paid £3.18s.1d. Exceptions to bales of rubber and casks of oil were drums of acetone, £4.15s; a ship's motor boat, £10; bundles of cork, £6.5s.3d; a signal flag, 4d; 1cwt of candle wax, 6s.7d and 118 gallons of claret, £7. 1s. 3d.

Rumours abounded on 12 October that the enemy had accepted President Wilson's terms for a cease-fire, which led to great speculation. The truth of the matter was that the German Chancellor, Prince Maximillian of Baden, had contacted US President Woodrow Wilson and requested an armistice based on Wilson's 14-point plan outlined the previous January. The Germans were advised that there could be no negotiations until the removal of the country's military leadership, so fighting continued. On 9 November Kaiser Wilhelm II abdicated, going into exile in the Netherlands the following day.

On 11 November, the Armistice on the Western Front, negotiated over four days in a railway carriage at Compiègne, finalized just six hours earlier, came into force at 11am, and the First World War officially came to an end. Hundreds of thousands of German troops had already either surrendered or had simply headed for home. The terms of the Armistice had been agreed between a delegation headed by the German politician Matthias Erzberger and Marshal Ferdinand Foch, Supreme Allied Commander in the final year of the war. The

Allies demanded nothing short of unconditional surrender, that German forces must immediately evacuate all occupied territory; surrender substantial amounts of military supplies including 5,000 heavy artillery pieces and 25,000 machine guns; evacuate German territory west of the River Rhine; allow three zones on the east bank of the Rhine to be occupied; surrender all its submarines and intern all other warships at ports indicated by the Allies. Admiral Sir David Beatty accepted the surrender of the German High Seas fleet on 21 November, his message to them was unambiguous, 'The German flag will be hauled down at sunset and will not be hoisted again without permission. The Fleet will move to anchorages at Scapa Flow in the Orkneys off the coast of Northern Scotland.'

Whilst the Armistice ended the First World War, it did not bring peace to Europe, since fighting immediately broke out in the former provinces of Russia and Austria-Hungary over territorial demands of the newly independent states of Eastern Europe.

The basic statistics concerning the war are staggering. The German Navy lost 178 U-boats, along with 515 officers and 4,894 ratings. Overall 65 million troops were mobilized worldwide, of whom 8 million were killed and 21 million wounded. Germany lost 1.8 million soldiers, Austria-Hungary 922,000; France 1.36 million; the British Empire 908,000; Russia 1.7 million and the USA 150,000. An estimated 6.6 million civilians lost their lives, countless millions of others going to their graves carrying deep physical or mental scars.

On Scilly, at the 11th hour of the 11th day of the 11th month of 1918, a Monday, flags were hoisted all across the naval base, all the trawlers, drifters and tugs blowing their steam whistles, whilst bunting, flags and streamers, hidden away for four long years appeared throughout Hugh Town. On Tresco staff crawled across the rooftops with bunting, a Union Jack was flown from the Abbey's flagpole. There were bonfires and fireworks on every island.

The Isles of Scilly Council met on 5 December when it was proposed that the whole council form a committee for any festivities or celebrations of peace being declared, it was also proposed to erect or have made some fitting memorial to the islanders lost in the war. Alderman Bluett proposed that application be made to the War Office through Major A.A. Dorrien-Smith for some trophies of the war, a piece of German artillery or something captured from the enemy, to be presented to the islands. This was not unusual since many mainland councils had received war trophies as large as howitzer guns, even complete tanks, which went on display along with smaller weapons or similar souvenirs.

It was also reported to the council that the raised date of 1847 on the back of the stone at the end of the New Seat at the bottom of Telegraph Hill had recently been vandalized, the date chipped off by a man of the detachment of RAF at Holy Vale. The officer in charge expressed his regret and promised to have the date re-cut at the culprit's expense. It was proposed that the date numbers should be raised.

A fitting end to 1918 is perhaps this delightful little verse written by Chief Petty Officer F.J. Tadman of RNAS/RAF Tresco, the man who clambered out onto the wing of his damaged seaplane and stuffed his handkerchief into a hole in the cooling fluid tank, saving both the aircraft and the lives of his crew. This poem was found in the 1917 autograph book of Kathleen M. Lethbridge. Thanks to Kay and John Banfield for permission to use it:

How doth the little German sub
Improve each shining day?
By sinking every unarmed tub
That dares to come her way.
How brave the crew, they launch their torp
And while the wreckage tosses,
They hasten back to Kaiser Bill
To get their Iron Crosses.

30 May 1917

CHAPTER 6

1919 onward
We Will Remember Them

Slowly, some of the many aspects of war that affected the Isles of Scilly were wound down or ceased to function following the November Armistice. The Government rescinded the Conscription Act and by early 1919 the RNAPS base had virtually closed down. The trawlers and drifters returned to Royal Dockyards where they were given back to their original owners, many continuing to fish for another twenty-one years until the Second World War, when many of the same craft were requisitioned for a second period of war service. The trawlers, drifters and tugs that were still at Scilly on 11 November 1918 were:

Trawlers – *Cambria, City of Edinburgh, Foss, Hercules IV, Imelda, Isaac Chant, Nancy Hague, Raindrop, Saurian, Thomas Graham, Thomas Hanking, Whitefriars.*
Drifters: *Laurel III, Marvellous, Rambling Rose.*
Rescue tugs: *Blazer, Bramley Moore, Cynic, Epic, Resolve, Revenger, Woonda.*

Ironically, the rescue tug *Blazer*, which had done such sterling work throughout the war was herself wrecked the day before the Armistice in an unfortunate accident, less than a mile from her berth alongside the quay at St Mary's. She had been in Penzance following a towing job when her crew heard of the impending Armistice which would come into force the very next day, so her captain requested permission from Falmouth to return to Scilly that night. On entering St Mary's Sound around midnight she passed inside of the Woolpack rock, went aground and her engine room commenced to fill. With a heavy sea running, a strong tide and the tug's engine running full astern she was refloated only to sink south of Davis's Ledge. About half of the crew of twenty-eight managed to get into her one small boat, the remainder now in the sea fighting for their lives and battling a mass of floating fenders and deck gear. Fortunately, the captain had let off several rockets and flares before taking to the boat which were seen by skipper Joe Pender of Trot Boat No.9, the duty boat alongside the quay awaiting any orders. Expecting to hear from the duty lieutenant on board the drifter *Marvellous* at any moment, the Trot Boat's boiler was fired up and the crew prepared for sea, but no orders came. So using his initiative, the skipper cast off and was close to Steval Point and the casualty within ten minutes, where they met a mass

Joseph Henry Pender, known as 'Joe', who was coxswain of the Trot Boat. This served the armed vessels outside the harbour on moorings, by carrying men, mail and stores. Joe was the hero of the tug *Blazer* incident who put to sea on his own initiative and saved the tug's crew. *(St Mary's Museum, Isles of Scilly)*

of floating wreckage. By now coastguards had been alerted and were on the Garrison shore, shouting to the survivors not to try and swim ashore since it was far too dangerous in the heavy swell. In the meantime the crew of the Trot Boat were dragging men out of the sea who were sent below into the engine room for warmth. Then

Aerial view of RNAS/RAF Tresco showing extent of the naval air base. *(St Mary's Museum, Isles of Scilly)*

the *Blazer*'s boat was found and its fourteen men rescued, after which they headed for the harbour, passing the St Mary's lifeboat on its way to the rescue, along with trawlers and drifters.

The duty lieutenant who should have been down on the quay that night later said to Joe Pender, 'Mum's the word', no doubt having been in Tregarthen's Hotel celebrating instead of being on the quay. So the fact the lieutenant had not been where he should have been, and that the Trot Boat was taken to sea without orders was quietly forgotten. A letter from the crew of the tug was sent to Joe Pender and his two men dated 11 November 1918, which read:

> *'On behalf of the Blazer's officers and men please accept the accompaniment of this note as our very small appreciation of valuable services rendered. You undoubtedly saved our lives and we offer you our heartiest thanks. Signed: H. Barker – for all'.*

HM Tug *Blazer*, which sank at St Mary's on Armistice night, returning from Penzance. Note that she is armed with a bow gun. *(Mike Harcum Collection)*

The premises occupied by the RNAPS on the quay were handed back to the Duchy of Cornwall. The White House, Tregarthen's Hotel, Holgate's Hotel, Lemon Hall, Ennor House and many others, ceased to be military hospitals and billets, and the Army, Navy and Air Force Club in the church hall closed as the islands returned to something like normal. RAF Tresco remained as it was, busy with trials and development of new ideas, equipment and weapons until May 1919 when 234 Anti-Submarine Squadron was disbanded, a total of eight aircrew having lost their lives in the conflict. There had been much deliberation in the War Office as to whether Tresco should remain a permanent seaplane base after the war, but this was discounted on the grounds of economy. However, a number of wartime bases remained serviceable and earmarked for continued experimental flights and trials, Tresco included, and to this end it was to be used up to the end of 1922.

In August that year, a Short F-5 seaplane used the base for a while, and that same month a prototype of the new Short Cromarty

The Short Cromarty N120 seaplane that came to Tresco after the war for trials, was damaged after hitting a shoal, and is shown here beached in St Mary's harbour. *(St Mary's Museum, Isles of Scilly)*

N-120, on trials from the RAF Seaplane Development Flight at Felixstowe came to Scilly, flown by Squadron Leader R. Maycock OBE, who had been in command of RAF Tresco in 1917. Whilst here the aircraft proved it was capable of riding out a severe storm in St Mary's Roads, but was later accidentally taxied onto a shallow reef where it sank up to its lower wings. They somehow managed to taxi it to St Mary's harbour where it was beached, but beyond economic repair it was broken up.

HMS *Ark Royal*, a seaplane carrier used as a depot ship to follow the N120 trial flight along the coast from Felixstowe, via Newhaven, Calshot, Torbay, Mount Batten, Plymouth to Scilly and back, came to St Mary's and salvaged the remains of the aircraft. Other flying boats, an F3, a Kingston and a Felixstowe F5 (NJ4839), which had accompanied the Cromarty N-120, all returned from Scilly safely. Whilst RAF Tresco was still in use, a letter from its medical officer to the council concerning a well on the island stated that

Another aerial view of the Tresco seaplane base before the large steel hangar was built. *(Fleet Air Arm Museum, Yeovil)*

The RNAS/RAF Tresco seaplane base being demolished in 1923. (*St Mary's Museum, Isles of Scilly*)

examination of the water by the Clinical Research Association, showed that chemically and bacteriologically the water was polluted. The council understandably proposed that the Air Ministry be asked to have the well cleaned out, since it was their sole responsibility, seemingly unaware that Major Dorrien-Smith had taken over from the Air Ministry the liability of all the wells on Tresco. The major asked if the requirements of the council would be met if after cleaning, a stand-pipe was fixed free of charge to the present water service laid down by the RAF for the supply of drinking water.

This arm of the services, the RAF, which started as the Royal Flying Corps (RFC) on 13 May 1912, became the Royal Naval Air Service (RNAS) from 1 July 1914, then the Royal Air Force (RAF) on 1 April 1918, eventually the Fleet Air Arm (FAA) from 1 April 1924, but by then the air station at Tresco had closed completely. The 26-acre premises were handed back to Tresco Estate, which had the large hangar dismantled, but made good use of some of the remaining smaller buildings. The wooden slipway which had seen the launch and recovery of hundreds of flying boats, slowly rotted away to be replaced later by a smaller, narrower concrete slip which still survives. At the head of the slipway now stands the Flying Boat Club, a popular restaurant and bar, whose walls hold many photographs as a tribute to the work of the old air station in the Great War.

The War Memorial in Old Town churchyard. It was dedicated and unveiled in May 1921 by HRH the Prince of Wales, Duke of Cornwall. *(St Mary's Museum, Isles of Scilly)*

The War Memorial in Tresco churchyard. *(Richard Larn Collection)*

In March 1919 the Council of the Isles of Scilly again considered a memorial in honour of Scillonians who had lost their lives in the war, and agreed that a public meeting should be held on 25 March. The Council recommended that a monument should be erected on the Parade or on the Strand, on the site of an old blacksmith's shop alongside the Rechabite slipway, on which suitable tablets bearing the men's names be inscribed. An earlier suggestion had been to erect a war memorial outside the main church, in the centre of the junction of the two roads, creating an island, but an influential Scillonian who had lost a son in the war objected, on the grounds that every time he went past the junction he would be reminded of his loss. In addition, a suitable brass tablet bearing names should be erected inside each church on the off-islands.

The Roll of Honour in the parish church on St Mary's was the gift of Mrs Addison, wife of Dr Addison who worked tirelessly for the islands from 1912 till 1927. This was a cardboard mounted record, which was replaced by a carved wooden roll in 1926. It was an incredible **two years after the Armistice**, when the council resolved that the proposed 'United Memorial Service for the Fallen in the last War' should be held in the parish church the following Sunday, attended by the entire council. Certainly, there seemed no great hurry either to erect a war memorial, since council minutes of 31 March 1921, twenty-eight months after Armistice Day, stated that an application be made for a faculty for the erection of the war memorial in the churchyard at Old Town. For whatever reason, peace celebrations were still being discussed on 5 July 1919, when it was

A recruiting poster printed in the *Royal Cornwall Gazette* newspaper in 1915 made promises that were never kept. *(Richard Larn Collection)*

resolved that a public tea should be provided for adults and children when each child should each receive a commemorative medal. The clerk also reported that a letter had been received from Messrs. Hain & Company, of St Ives, who ran the ferry, requesting payment of £300, the wartime subsidy for running the SS *Artificer* between the islands and the mainland for the period 15 December 1917 to 15 June 1919, and drew the attention of the company to the fact that £150 had already been paid.

Alderman Bluett's suggestion on 5 December 1918 regarding war trophies appears to have borne fruit at some earlier date, since on 2 September 1919 the council suggested that the two German trench mortars be placed in one of the Garrison batteries. It was also proposed that the German guns received be moved from the Parade to the Garrison, if no objection was raised by the Divisional Officer of Coastguards. Other matters concerned the chairman's endeavours to induce the Postmaster General to establish a permanent Wireless Telegraphy Station on the islands, having stated he was not unfavourable to the scheme. The council also gave an undertaking to do its best to find employment for disabled ex-servicemen to the amount of 5 per cent of the council's total staff, but there are no records of how many servicemen returned to Scilly disabled, blinded or suffering from shell-shock. The recruiting posters in 1914-15 had been ebullient about the honour and glory of fighting for one's King and Country. One poster stated that:

'After the War every man who has served will command his Country's gratitude. He will be looked up to and respected because he answered his country's call. The Regiments at the Front are covering themselves with Glory.'

In 1919 as millions of men were discharged and returned to their home towns, cities and communities, they found themselves in a completely different world to the one they had left. A world which did not want to know about their suffering, their sacrifice or their wounds, a world in which women were now doing the jobs of men, a world which offered them mostly unemployment, leaving many with no option but to beg or peddle matches on the streets, openly displaying the stumps of missing arms or wooden legs hoping for sympathy. It was not the world they had been promised, had fought for, or expected on their return.

Following surrender of the U-boat fleet, *UB-101* was taken into Newlyn harbour in and opened up to the public. *(Penlee House Gallery & Museum, Percy Sharp Collection)*

Inside the torpedo room of the German U-boat brought into Newlyn harbour. *(Penlee House Gallery & Museum, Percy Sharp Collection)*

The Isles of Scilly appear to have lost 46 local men of over 500 who served during the war, just under 10 per cent, but that figure may not be accurate. The main war memorial in Old Town churchyard on St Mary's is presumed to hold the names of all who lost their lives on active service regardless of which island they came from. However, there are also individual off-island war memorials in the churchyards on St Agnes, Bryher, Tresco and St Martin's which record the names of men from those islands, and in theory the numbers should add up, but unfortunately do not. The names on the individual memorials show: Bryher – 1; St Agnes – 2; St Martin's – 3 and Tresco – 48, which total 54.

Taking just one individual as an example, Frederick Jenkins, Life Guards, died at Ypres, on 16 November 1914; his name appears on

The forward 10cm (4-inch) deck gun on the surrendered German submarine *UB-101*, with Royal Navy officers trying out its controls (see p.46). *(Penlee House Gallery & Museum, Percy Sharp Collection)*

This photograph is a mystery. It shows very young boys dressed in white Royal Navy tropical uniform, practising semaphore signalling on the beach by Old Quay steps, St Mary's under the stern of a large vessel. There is a man dressed in navy 'square-rig' (back, left) who may be a Coastguard. The question is, what was this organisation? They are not CLB. *(St Mary's Museum)*

the Tresco memorial, but does not show on the main St Mary's memorial. There is a Frederick Jennings named at Old Town, but is this the same man? Did the stonemason make a spelling mistake, or is it someone else? A project is under way as a result of this book on behalf of the recently formed Isles of Scilly Branch of the British Legion, to record what is believed to be the names of over 500 men and women from the islands who served in the Great War, whose names should be on the Roll of Honour. Only then can we determine exactly each individual's unit, rank, how many of these lost their lives and if so, their date of death and place of burial, if known.

The Great War is particularly poignant for me, the author. My father, Major Cyril Francis Larn was Commanding Officer of the 47th Battalion, Machine Gun Corps, who served at the front for four years including Mons, Ypres and both battles of the Somme. Mentioned in despatches several times and seriously wounded prior to 1918, at the second battle of the Somme he was awarded a Military Cross. He remained in the army until 1923, then was invalided out suffering from PTSD (Post Traumatic Stress Disorder) or shell-shock as it was known in those days. In 1931 he took his own life consequently, being only eighteen months old at the time, I never knew him. On Armistice Day each year, I wear his Military Cross with pride.

'Why are they selling poppies, Mummy?
Selling poppies in town today.
The poppies, child, are flowers of love.
For the men who marched away.

But why have they chosen a poppy, Mummy?
Why not a beautiful rose?
Because my child, men fought and died
In the fields where the poppies grow.

But why are the poppies so red, Mummy?
Why are the poppies so red?
Red is the colour of blood, my child.
The blood that our soldiers shed.

The heart of the poppy is black, Mummy
Why does it have to be black?
Black, my child, is the symbol of grief.
For the men who never came back.

But why, Mummy, are you crying so?
Your tears are giving you pain.
My tears are my fears for you my child.
For the world is forgetting again.

Anzac Day Commemorative Committee
Author unknown

Bibliography

Adams, F.&P., *Star Castle and Its Garrison*. Belvedere Press, 1984

Auten, H., *Q-Boat Adventures*. Herbert Jenkins, 1925

Bowley, R.L., *Scilly at War*. Bowley Publications Ltd, 2001

Campbell, G., *My Mystery Ships*. Hodder & Stoughton Ltd, 1923

Chatterton, E.K., *Beating the U-Boats*. Anchor Press, 1943

Chatterton, E.K., *Q-Ships and their Story*. Conway Maritime Press Ltd, 1972

Chatterton, E.K., *Fighting the U-Boats*. Hurst & Blackett Ltd, 1942

Gill, C., *The Duchy of Cornwall*. David & Charles, 1987

Goodall, M.H., *Cross & Cockade International Journal,*. Vol 19, No.1, 1988

Jameson, W., *The Most Formidable Thing*. Rupert Hart-Davis Ltd, 1965

Kloot, W. van der., *World War 1 Fact Book*. Amberley Publishing Plc, 2001

Llewellyn, S., *Emperor Smith – the Man who Built Scilly*. The Dovecote Press, 2005

London, P., *Cornwall in the First World War*. Truran/Tor Mark Press. 2013

London, P., *U-Boat Hunters*. Dyllansow Truran, 1999

Osborne, J.P., *Scillonian War Diary 1914-18, Vols. 1 – 3,* unpublished

Westwell, I., *World War One Day by Day*. Grange Books Plc, 2000

Index